Star of India
THE LOG OF AN IRON SHIP

In silent dignity, the 113-year-old *Star of India* made sail off San Diego Bay on July 4, 1976. The climax to her brief cruise came when she sailed back into the harbor without help from the tugs, rounded up into the wind and let go the anchor off B Street Pier. — PHOTO BY ROSCOE SMITH

STAR OF INDIA
THE LOG OF AN IRON SHIP

by Jerry MacMullen

with Foreword by
CAPTAIN ALAN VILLIERS

Howell-North • 1961 • Berkeley, California

Printed and bound in the United States of America.

Library of Congress Catalogue Card No. 61-18614

ISBN 0-8310-7027-7

First Printing, 1961
Second Printing, 1966
Third (Revised) Printing, 1973
Fourth (Revised) Printing, 1978

Published by Howell-North Books
1050 Parker Street, Berkeley, California 94710

CONTENTS   ★   ★   ★   ★   ★   ★   ★

LIST OF ILLUSTRATIONS ★ ★ ★ ★ ★ ★ ★

To the memory of a Jovial Giant,
and a Superb Seaman

CAPTAIN FRANK WEIDEMANN
Last Master of the Bark *Star of India*

He was good to his sailors

★   ★   ★

I AM PLEASED TO WRITE A BRIEF FOREWORD FOR JERRY MAC-Mullen's story of the good ship *Star of India, ex-Euterpe*. It is the Port of San Diego's privilege that the old ship chose that beautiful harbor for her last lay-up. What chance gave to them, now the citizens are going to preserve, and it is a grand thing that this should be so. It was ships such as this and their rugged, minute (by modern standards) hard-sailing predecessors which opened up the trade routes of the world, which made all the great discoveries, which fought most of the decisive sea battles.

We are the last generation to which the art and science of handling them, and with it a true understanding of them, may be handed down. We are the last and there will be no more, for such ships are gone. It behooves us, therefore, to do what we can to preserve all forms of knowledge of these deep-sea sailing ships while it still may be done — and, above all, to hold on, here and there, to such few as by good fortune still survive. Here and there, a handful may still be found — in the Baltic ports of Stockholm and Mariehamn, the ship *af Chapman* and the four-masted barque *Pommern;* in Gothenburg, the four-masted barque *Viking;* in West Germany, the four-masted barque *Passat;* in the port of London, the clipper *Cutty Sark;* in San Francisco, the ship *Balclutha;* in the U.S.S.R., the four-masted barques *Padua* and *Magdalene Vinnen,* renamed and used as training ships; in Portugal the barque *Sagres* and in Spain the *Galatea,* both elderly Cape Horners, still in use as training ships.

But the *Star of India* is the doyen of all these — almost a century old! What a record! Metal ships were not intentionally built to last that long. Indeed, in 1863 when she was

8

built at Ramsey in the Isle of Man — a holiday island in the Irish Sea, with its own parliament and great traditions — nobody knew how long they might be good for, and there were still sceptics who held that iron ships would not float at all. So they built them solid and they built them good. Good iron looked after may be made to last almost forever. Stout iron plates and iron wire rigging have shown themselves to be remarkably durable, nowhere more so than in the *Star of India*. For sixty years she roamed the highways of the seven seas, round the Horn and round the Cape, running her Easting Down (as sailors used to say) in violent gales, sweltering in the Doldrums calm on the Line, nudging the ice aside with her sharp iron cutwater in cold Alaskan seas. On 22 round voyages, she carried immigrants to New Zealand — a long, hard haul outwards from England — for Shaw Saville's, a famous British shipping line. Jute from India, sugar from Hawaii, lumber from Puget Sound filling the huge hold and piled high on the main deck, coal for San Francisco, canned salmon by the thousand cases for that same port for the famed Alaska Packers' Line — all these cargoes she safely delivered. All these hard voyages she safely made, without fuss, with little bother, almost without incident — just an old iron "windjammer" going quietly and efficiently about her share of the world's sea-borne trade. And finally the winds blew her to San Diego, where she is — I hope — to see her second century out, an inspiring relic of a great age, when strong wind blew in her stout rigging and men knew how to make effective use of it for the delivery of passengers and cargoes over long voyages at sea.

Well, her story is here. Jerry MacMullen — Director of the Junípero Serra Museum and president of the San Diego Maritime Museum Association — is the man to write it. He has done a fine job.　　　　　ALAN VILLIERS

September 28, 1961
"Windrush," Oxford

9

ACKNOWLEDGMENTS ★ ★ ★ ★ ★ ★ ★

Compiling the history of *Star of India* has been an all-hands job; had it not been for the cheerful and enthusiastic assistance of many people who wished her well, her story never would have been told.

William R. Sarjeant, Librarian-Archivist for the Manx Museum, must have turned the Isle of Man topsy-turvy in search for vital items, as did F. A. Hawkes, Shipping Editor for Lloyd's of London, and O. C. Wright of the office of the Registrar General of Shipping and Seamen, at Cardiff, Wales. In San Francisco Jack McNairn, at the time pursuing old shellbacks with his tape recorder for the Maritime Museum's files, and Karl Kortum, director of that superb museum, were twin towers of strength. Jumping back to England, Captain Alan Villiers lent sage counsel which included the admonition not to forget the Alaska Packers, and to "put in a plug for *Balclutha!*"

The ship's old owners, Shaw, Savill & Albion, were kind and helpful from their offices in London and in New Zealand. So were our own National Archives and Record Service at Washington, D. C., and the Bancroft Library of the University of California, at Berkeley. The brazen manner in which *Euterpe* played fast and loose with the laws of two nations came to light through the kindly cooperation of James P. Winne, Collector of Customs and Agnes C. Conrad, State Archivist, at Honolulu, Hawaii, who really "made a Federal case of it."

Veterans of the frozen north like Lieutenant Commander M. A. Ransom USCG (Ret.), and Captains Clifford and

10

Otto Weidemann — son and nephew respectively of her last master — were most helpful in the fields of fact and photography. Letters to Harold D. Huycke, merchant marine officer and maritime historian par excellence, brought airmail replies from everywhere between New York and Yokohama, wherever his ship chanced to be.

The might of the Fourth Estate was unleashed in the quest for data by Abe Mellinkoff, City Editor of *The San Francisco Chronicle* and Leonard H. Verbarg, Sunday "Knave" Editor of *The Oakland Tribune;* and Bert Shankland brought rare photographic skill into play in reproducing pages from those faded, water-stained old logbooks, filched from the Packers' files so long ago by "Sweetheart Jack" Brunnick.

In his cozy home "out in the avenues" of San Francisco, Captain Carl J. Carlson leaned back in his armchair and recalled fan-tan games, knife fights, a macabre funeral and an incipient tong war in *Star of India* — and left an uneasy feeling that here, perhaps, was the man who should be writing the book himself. Phil Middlebrook of San Diego turned a long-dreamed-of vacation voyage to New Zealand into a dedicated round of such repositories of lore as The Alexander Turnbull Library at Wellington, and steamship offices there and elsewhere.

And there were others; quiet old men with stars and anchors tattooed on the backs of their gnarled hands, who sat behind windows of their own little Snug Harbors or on sunny benches in Alameda, trying pathetically to bring back into focus a lusty era which we will never see again.

A fair wind to you all!

JERRY MacMULLEN

San Diego, California
1961

11

Part 1   Under the Red Duster

CHAPTER I

A COLD COLLATION IS SERVED

YOU CAN'T BEAT SATURDAY AS A LAUNCHING DAY. SHIPYARD workers have been known to celebrate a successful launching not wisely but too well, and having the affair on a Saturday enables them to sober up on their own time. All of this may or may not have been why Saturday, November 14, 1863, was chosen for that festive day at the yard of Messrs. Gibson, McDonald & Arnold at Ramsey, in the far-off Isle of Man.

On the stocks was the naked hull of an iron ship, awaiting the dollop of baptismal wine across her forefoot. Among the flags which dressed the sleek iron hull, three stood out smartly — the British Union Jack, the colors of the Port of Liverpool and, for reasons which are not entirely clear, the Stars and Stripes. And in this pretty gesture there was something prophetic, for it was the American flag, last of the three under which she was fated to sail, which was to carry her, renamed *Star of India,* to the end of her first century afloat.

Above the platform which had been rigged for the launching party, her figurehead gazed serenely over the crowd; it was a buxom figure of the Greek goddess Euterpe, fresh from the skillfully plied chisels of George Sutherland, the Glasgow carver. That was to be her name — *Euterpe* — and that figurehead was to scan the rolling greybacks of the Roaring Forties, the pack ice of the Bering Sea, and the waterfronts of, to name but a few, Calcutta, Melbourne, Wellington and San Francisco. Most of that figurehead is intact today, and whether the few missing bits were lost to a nameless Spanish brig off the Welsh coast, to the steamship *Canadian* in Glasgow or to the plodding stern-wheeler *Fort Bragg* in San Francisco is not a matter of record.

As busy as a beaver that day was the reporter from the Manx newspaper *Mona's Herald;* he was going to have to fill the equivalent of three columns of agate type, so it is small wonder that he went into some detail.

"A large number of ladies and gentlemen," he wrote, "were present at the yard in order to witness the launching of the ship, amongst whom were — the Hon. and Right Rev. The Lord Bishop and Miss Powis, His Worship the High Bailiff and Mrs. Tellett, Thomas Cummings Gibson, Esq., Captain McDonald, E. R. Arnold, Esq., Captain Brown, Mrs. Brown, Captain Thornley Gibson . . . Colonel Thellusson, Rev. C. M. S. Mules . . . Rev. T. B. Lee . . . Captain Thellusson . . . Dr. Clucas . . . the Misses Gilders . . . &c, &c."

"At the bow of the ship a platform was erected for the purpose of enabling Mrs. Brown (the lady upon whom the pleasing ceremony of christening the ship devolved) to baptize her effectually by means of a bottle of port wine . . . Captain McDonald having given the command — "Out shores," the piece of timber familiarly called "the dagger" was withdrawn. The ship then began to move slowly down the ways, and Mrs. Brown, seizing the bottle of wine, dashed it against the stem of the vessel and said, 'I christen this gallant ship Euterpe.' The Euterpe, at ten minutes past twelve o'clock, noon, glided majestically into her future element . . ."

With that much of it accomplished, all hands settled down to the simple pleasures of the day. If it developed into anything like a modern launching with many bottles beside the baptismal one, and with two or three good fights underway simultaneously among the workmen, there was no mention of it in *Mona's Herald,* which went on thus:

14

"Immediately after the Euterpe had been safely moored in her berth, a cold collation was served in the sail room of the yard. The room was hung with flags, and presented a neat appearance. The luncheon was prepared by Miss Mylrea, of the Royal Hotel, Ramsey; and was well served, the edibles giving satisfaction and the wines being of excellent flavor . . ."

The ensuing speeches were long, and not particularly sprightly; they were, moreover, confined chiefly to the remarks of one W. Callister, Esq., the Chairman of the Day, and the Lord Bishop, on a sort of dialogue basis. There were toasts to Queen Victoria and to the local clergy, to the economic future of Ramsey and to Messrs. Wakefield, Nash & Company, East India merchants, of Tower Buildings, Water Street, Liverpool; they were *Euterpe's* owners, and Manxmen to boot.

Along around Toast Seven, the Lord Bishop was in fine trim, and so was Mr. Callister, who made the innocent but unfortunate remark that ". . . if Your Lordship will preach in the open air, or in any buildings on these premises, you will have a large congregation." In those days, one had to be careful about being identified with chaps who went about preaching in the open air, and the bishop was alert to the situation.

"I am afraid," he replied with dignity, "of Mr. Callister's remarks getting forth to the public; and that it may appear that I covet the position of an open air preacher. This I do not desire. But what I desire is to speak to the workmen as a workman . . . one as who, if I removed my silk apron and substituted a leather one for it, could make a screw equal to any of them."

Fortunately for posterity, the *Herald* reporter was able to emerge from the torrent of verbiage with enough strength left to record some good, solid technical details — priceless for those who undertook *Euterpe's* restoration nearly a century later. He listed her as an iron ship with full poop and fo'c'sle, and of 1246 tons register; she was 202 feet long on the keel, with a beam of 35 and a depth of 23½ feet. Her saloon cabin was 30 feet long, 15 feet wide at the forward end, and of 7 feet headroom. On each side of the cabin there were, originally, eight staterooms as well as a bath and toilet. Interior trim was — and still is — walnut with maple mouldings, and ". . . The stateroom doors are fitted with patent Venetian ventilators, of the same style as that adopted in the Peninsula and Oriental Company's steamers; additional ventilation is freely admitted by means of patent perforated zinc, which is placed along the entire length of the cabin, just above the stateroom doors."

At one point, however, he seems to have gone off the deep end; this was in the matter of her military potentialities. "On this (the main) deck," he wrote, "there are eight portholes which can be used for working guns of large calibre — thus, in case of necessity, the ship could be easily transformed into a ship of war, or used as a transport for the conveyance of troops." Obviously, he was referring to the wash ports, put there for no more belligerent purpose than freeing the deck of the tons of water which she was bound to ship in heavy weather.

The original deckhouse was 34 feet long, 14 feet wide, and 7 feet 9 inches high; the galley was at its forward end, and abaft of this important compartment were 14 berths for the "petty-officers and midshipmen." The fo'c'sle, right in the eyes of the ship, was 30 feet long, 7 feet high, and contained berths for 25 men. There are indications that, at some later date, the quarters for the 'fore-mast hands were located at the extreme forward end of the 'tweendecks; this space is provided not only with glass ports in the sides, but with a ventilator — of sorts.

16

Whether the original owners intended to make a trooper out of her, or were looking forward to emigrant ship potentialities, is unknown, but it is obvious that the 'tweendecks was intended for human cargo. Some 30 ports, with "patent covers," were provided, and fittings for the slinging of hammocks were noted as well. It was estimated that she could carry 600 troops.

Decking of poop and main deck was, originally, of red pine, added strength at the sides being given by wide strakes of greenheart. Three capstans were located on the main deck, both these and the main pump (still in place) being supplied by John Wilson, of Liverpool. The weather side of the poop bulkhead was of teak, as were the skylight and the rails. Mooring bitts on poop and main deck were of novel design, in that their tops could be removed, to admit air to the staterooms and 'tweendecks.

It appears that the captain's cabin, originally, was on the starboard side, at the forward end of the poop. The mate's was on the port side, each opening onto a short alleyway between the poop bulkhead and the forward end of the main cabin. In the center, between these two alleyways, were the pantry and what was described as a combined chart room and library, and there were four plate glass windows, with appropriate storm covers, in the poop bulkhead, through which the officers could keep an eye on the men. It is likely that one window each was in the captain's and the mate's room, and two in the chart room. What in later years became the captain's cabin, away aft, originally seems to have been the sail locker. It is obvious today that there have been many changes in the after part of the vessel.

The cabin skylight, 16 feet long and of teak and brass, was fitted originally as it is today, with seats on each side of the glass — a common practice in sailing vessels. Painted on glass at the after end there still exists a well executed

17

picture of Euterpe herself; at the forward end, originally, was a painting of the arms of the Port of Liverpool. Both were from the Liverpool glass works of Forrest & Company. The forward one has long since vanished, being replaced by solid planks.

Lower masts were of iron, just as they are today — with the exception of the mizzen; when, years later, she was cut down to a bark, a wooden mizzenmast was installed. Her sails were supplied by David Corsar & Son, of Glasgow, and contained some 15,000 yards of soft, gray-white flax. A painting in the possession of the Manx Museum, at Douglas, reveals that, originally, she was rigged for a main skys'l yard.

Those who feel that *Euterpe* looked old for her years are not being wholly unreasonable. Even as she lay, spanking new, at her builders' wharf, there was something about her that seemed quaint and old-fashioned. For one thing, her hull had very little sheer — which made her, when she got into heavy weather, a pretty wet ship. With a low fo'c'sle and a low poop, seas came aboard her forward and they came aboard her aft, and her log books are well larded with entries about her deck being full of water as she slogged her way through the seas, rather than over them.

Below the waterline as well as above, her bows are a bit on the pudgy side — nor are the lines of her after part exactly what you would call yacht-like. It almost seems as if her builders hesitated to discard the full-bodied lines of the grand old East Indiamen, and refused to believe that the clipper ship was here to stay. Well — if they didn't want a "flash packet" they must have been well satisfied, for she was certainly no record breaker. Although she continued to haul cargo and people for a great many years, and no doubt made money for her owners, she took her own sweet time about it. In her later colonial service she never made it to New

Zealand in under 100 days, although others such as *Turakina* and *Peter Denny* at times got there in 80 or less.[1]

Instead of what by then had become the traditional pair of poop ladders, one to starboard and one to port, *Euterpe* had, one might say, a sort of grand staircase. Access to her poop from the main deck was by a single, massive set of teak steps, bound in brass, right on the centerline. True enough, when *Cromdale* and *Mount Stewart* came out in the early 1890s, they had single poop ladders; just the same, it was getting old fashioned, even in 1863.

Turnbuckles were already known in *Euterpe's* time, but they were not for her. Honest dead-eyes of lignum vitae, set up by hemp lanyards and well doused with Stockholm tar, were what were to keep her rigging taut.

For many years, there have been those who commented sourly upon an awkward gap between the bottom of her bowsprit and the top of her figurehead. Under a powerful magnifying glass, a photograph of 1874 revealed no such gap; the space was filled with a form of decoration sometimes called "hair rails," gracefully curved boards which swept aft from the figurehead to the bow plating, just below bulwark level. It's a fitting which goes back to the eighteenth century, and calls to mind the decoration of even earlier ships. The photo explained an old mystery in the form of an iron bolt, right in between Mrs. Euterpe's shoulders; it held the forward ends of these rails. Where the after ends were secured was revealed in 1960 when they sandblasted off the old paint. There were the marks on her plates where the after ends had been fastened.[2]

During the flowery speeches that November afternoon, a hint was dropped that in three weeks she would be ready

---

[1] Brett, Henry: *White Wings;* Auckland, N. Z., 1924

[2] Also revealed by this sandblasting were her Plimsoll marks, and the original draft numerals.

for sea. The prediction was not too far off, for on Wednesday, December 23 *Mona's Herald* said:

"The new ship Euterpe which was launched a short time since from the Ramsey shipbuilding yard, was towed to Liverpool by the tugboat Royal Arch on Thursday last. The Euterpe was removed from her moorings at the shipyard wharf on Monday, and placed alongside the North Pier to await the arrival of the tugboat from Liverpool. The tug not having arrived on Thursday, the Euterpe was taken in tow on Thursday afternoon by the steamer Mona's Isle, Captain Skillicorn, and safely towed into the bay, where the ship came to an anchor. As the Euterpe passed the pierhead, with masts and rigging complete, and some of her sails bent, a large number of spectators who had assembled on the Pier to witness her departure, cheered vociferously. The tugboat arrived in Ramsey Bay during Thursday night, and having taken the Euterpe in tow, proceeded to Liverpool, where both vessels safely arrived on Friday."

So now she was gone, and Ramsey was not to see her again. She and her mates from that modest shipyard, the iron ships *Eurydice, Erato* and *Ramsey*, of roughly the same size, were to play their big or little parts in the commerce of the sea. Of that brave little quartet, only she was to survive to a ripe old age, in a port half way around the world from where she slid down the ways so long ago.

Ahead of her lay tropical seas, strange cargoes in strange and far-off ports, collisions, fire, strandings, the ice of Alaskan waters, and a score of globe-girdling voyages.

"THIS DAY WE ARRIVED IN TRINCOMALEE . . ."

WITH A ROUND FLOURISH, THE INSPECTORS SIGNED *Euterpe's* initial survey report on January 5, 1864, having duly noted those now fantastic 13⁄16″ plates from her garboards to the upper part of the bilge, together with all of her gear. There was appropriate comment upon her seaworthy condition and general excellence; they awarded her the classification of "Double A-1, with a Cross" — and who could ask for more than that?

The last of her cargo soon was aboard and the hatches were down; on January 9 she left Liverpool for Calcutta and trouble, although not in that order. Sails were loosed; the towline was let go and with a mournful salute from her whistle, the tug swung back toward port and *Euterpe* was on her own for the first time.

With a new and untried ship under his feet, Captain William John Storry was on deck continuously for the first few days. Finally, at the point of exhaustion, he lay down on the cabin sofa during the early hours of January 13. He was fully clothed — which was fortunate, for his nap was to be but a brief one. The wind was light from the west southwest; stars were visible, but there was some haze on the horizon as *Euterpe* stood on into the night.

At 5 a.m., off St. David's Head, the lookout picked up a vessel with no lights, approaching off the port bow. Finding that his own running lights were in order, Second Officer Dowd, who had the watch, hailed the stranger and directed

21

her to pass astern of *Euterpe* — which, being close-hauled and the other vessel running free, had right-of-way. The hail was repeated twice without answer; then, seeing that a collision was inevitable, Mr. Dowd ordered the canvas thrown aback to check her headway, and sent for the master.

Captain Storry got on deck just as the crash came — at which time the stranger, a brig, thoughtfully hung out a red lantern. Up until then her decks seemed to have been deserted, and the only light visible to *Euterpe's* people had been the dim glow from her binnacle.

Aboard *Euterpe*, things were in a mess. Her jibboom had carried away, foresail and jibs were in tatters, and her tangled headgear was so fouled with the rigging of the brig that they could not get them apart. Captain Storry called repeatedly for the stranger's name, but, he reported, they ". . . spake in what I judged to be the Spanish language, so that I could not understand them." When they got clear, the brig kept on her course, heading for Holyhead. The crew of *Euterpe* busied themselves salvaging the shattered jibboom, clearing up the mess on deck, and then making sail to the westward.

"After making Sail on the Ship," reads Captain Storry's report of the affair, "the Crew came aft and desired to speak with me, on asking them what they wanted they replied that they desired me to put back into some Harbour, as the Ship was, in her disabled state, not fit to proceed to Sea, & as they was worn out with fatigue, it was impossible they could Work the Ship out of the Channel — I told them I was the best judge of that . . . we would try and repair damages & proceed on the Voyage — they replied that with all due deference to me, *they would not* proceed in the Ship, nor do any more Work unless I would bear up for some Harbour to put the ship in order . . .

"Seeing that they were obstinate, & that without the Crew being willing to Work, the ship was in danger, I consulted with my Officers, & finally concluded that, under the circumstances, we had no other alternative, but to put back, for the safety of the Ship & Cargo, as without men to work the Ship, she was in danger of being lost."

The following morning, with battered *Euterpe* heading back up St. George's Channel, the crew were mustered aft, and were asked if they would go on with the ship:

"They each & all answered that they would not do so, but would Stand by what they had first said — namely, that the Ship must go back, else, they would not Work."

The crew had won a victory, but an empty and costly one. Any thoughts that they were merely going to be taken back to Liverpool were of short duration. Two days later there was an entry in the log, and it wasn't signed by the master or the mate. It was signed by J. A. Williams and J. T. Roberts, two of Her Majesty's Justices of the Peace for the County of Anglesey, and it certified that *Euterpe's* seventeen sailors ". . . were this day committed by us to Beaumaris Gaol for Fourteen days with hard labour for refusing to proceed to Sea in the Ship 'Euterpe' bound on a Voyage from Liverpool to Calcutta." Repairs were made, and soon *Euterpe*, with a collision and a half-baked mutiny already in her little memory book, was on her way to Calcutta once more.

The round trip lasted eight months, and on November 15 she was back in Liverpool. It is possible that some of the alumni of her fo'c'sle (and of Beaumaris Gaol) bore her no particularly good will; while there is not a scrap of evidence to connect her next minor mishap with some disaffected sailor, at least it is interesting to find a small item a few days later in the Liverpool *Daily Courier:*

"A vessel on fire — In the course of Wednesday night a fire was discovered on board the Euterpe, from Calcutta, in the Queen's Dock; it was promptly extinguished, and very little damage was done."

A month and a half later, *Euterpe* found herself in London, whence she sailed on the last day of 1864, India-bound. It was fated to be her last voyage for Wakefield, Nash & Company — and Captain Storry's last voyage for anyone; he would never see England again. And once more violence was to be her lot; she was to meet disaster which far overshadowed her brush with the Spanish brig.

There are parts of the *Sailing Directions* which make grim reading, and these include the section devoted to the open roadstead of Madras, where *Euterpe* lay, in November of 1865. October is described as the most dangerous month, ". . . weather uncertain . . . cyclonic storms likely . . . a stormy sky should be heeded . . . November-December: Unsettled until early in December. Cyclonic storms often occur in November and even in early December. . . . During the prevalence of suspicious or threatening weather, the master of every vessel anchored within the limits of the roadstead is required not to be absent from his vessel between sunset and sunrise . . . and to maintain his vessel ready in every respect to proceed to sea on short notice . . ."

On November 23 the "suspicious" weather appeared, with ugly skies and a falling barometer. The situation deteriorated with such swiftness that there was no time to get in the anchor; *Euterpe* slipped her cable and stood out to sea, in the vain hope of escaping the onrushing gale.

For three terror-filled days she struggled on, trying to outrace the storm's hurricane force. Then the wind apparently shifted and caught her broadside. Over she went, further and further; those generous washports now were admitting the deluge to her flooded deck instead of dumping it overboard. Seas tore at her deck gear, at her hatches — and further down went her lee rail into the wind-torn foam.

24

Reluctantly Captain Storry gave the order to cut away her weather rigging, and let the masts and spars go by the board.

Now the hemp lanyards with which her rigging was set up, in place of the more up-to-date turnbuckles, stood her in good stead; the fibres gave way quickly to the axe blows, and with a thundering roar of rent canvas, snapping cordage and splintering wood, her topmasts and upper yards went over the side. Slowly, sluggishly, *Euterpe* got back on her feet, but she was dead in the water. Her crew, many of them hurt, now had the task of cutting away the tangled mess of gear which banged along her lee side.

With things as they were aboard, it is understandable that Captain Storry had little time left for the niceties of paper work, and so the details of their struggle to free the useless gear which clung to them, and to set up a jury rig of some kind, are lost to us. Apparently it was not until *Euterpe* again was making headway of sorts, and more or less answering her helm, that he found time to jot down a brief account:

"Nov. 23, 1865, Madras — This day we slipped from Madras to avoid an approaching Cyclone which unfortunately overtook us on the 26th & to save the Ship from foundering we was obliged to cut away the Masts, after which the sea broke over the Ship in terrible fury, Severly injuring a great portion of the Crew. With the remainder of the Crew we erected Jury masts & made the best of our way towards the land."

And then, under date of December 4:

"This day we arrived in [illegible] Bay, Trincomalie." [sic]

For three dismal months they lay at Trincomalee, patching up the ship — and themselves. A thorough inspection by Captain Storry and the mates and the carpenter showed that the iron hull was undamaged. There were letters to the owners, and letters from the underwriters, and plans to get her to some port where she would be rerigged; Calcutta was the nearest place.

A good deal of her rigging and canvas appeared to be usable. Whether they were unable to get a tug, or her owners (or master) were unduly frugal, is forgotten now; the fact remains that they decided to strengthen and improve their jury rig as much as possible, and try it under sail. So on March 5, 1866, she quitted Trincomalee under her own canvas, and ten days later she made Calcutta.

The stay in Calcutta, with its tropic heat and the annoyances and frustrations of refitting in a strange yard, thousands of miles from home, must have told heavily upon all hands, especially the master. And added to that, he picked up some sort of tropical fever which was shortly to prove fatal. Eight months had passed since their ordeal off Madras, when she cleared Calcutta for home on July 26 — with a dying man in command.

Light and baffling airs were all that they could find as *Euterpe* stood on slowly to the south, under the Bay of Bengal's sweltering heat. She was making good an average of only 65 miles a day, and on August 8, 1866, her noon position was Lat. 8° 30′ north, Long. 90° 29′ east. On that day, Captain Storry's troubles ended, the cause of his death being logged as "remittant fever." The main yards were backed, the ship was hove to and the Red Duster was lowered half way from the gaff. Chief Officer A. J. Whiteside read the service for burial at sea and with ". . . a sudden plunge to the sullen swell . . ." the weighted, canvas shrouded body was committed to the deep. The long voyage around the Cape of Good Hope and back to England continued, with Whiteside in command, and they reached Gravesend November 10.

Quite understandably, Messrs. Wakefield, Nash & Company had had enough of *Euterpe*, although there may have been factors other than their ship's dismantling and the loss of her master which led them to sell her. The new owner was David Brown, another East India merchant, who sent her to Calcutta on February 23, 1867. It was a rough passage out, and nearly three months after leaving England she still had not made the longitude of the Cape of Good Hope. Her new captain was having his problems, as witness the log for a wild day in mid-May of that year.

"May 19, 1867 — Lat 38° S. Long. 9° E. — Wind W.S.W. to W.N.W. Fresh breeze with heavy sea on.

"This day at noon commenced to throw part of the cargo overboard, in consequence of the behaviour of the Ship, during the late fearful hurricane we encountered as we considered it requisite & necessary for the safety of the ship, and the remainder of the cargo, to sacrifice a portion. — It is a positive fact that during the numerous passages that myself and the rest of the Crew have made round the Cape bound Eastwards at all times of the year we have never witnessed such a succession of Gales & such violent ones with so much sea on.

Wm. MURTON, (and others)
Master."

Captain Murton, who got her back to London on January 22, 1868, was but one of several who lasted for one voyage only — or perhaps could take it for only one trip.[1] Although many another ship behaved just as boisterously as she, life for the master of *Euterpe* seems to have been singularly lacking in dull moments. At that, her 1868, 1869 and 1870 voyages seem to have been without too much in the way of blood, sweat and tears, and it began to look as if she were beginning to settle down a bit.

----

[1]For a full list of masters, see Appendix.

CHAPTER III   ★   ★   ★   ★   ★   ★   ★

EMIGRANTS, COAL — AND BALLAST

BROWN KEPT HER ONLY FOR A MATTER OF FOUR YEARS OR SO. On October 3, 1871, she arrived at Le Havre from Bombay, on the first of her two visits to the European continent, and was sold to Shaw, Savill (later Shaw, Savill & Albion), then industriously building up a fleet whose house flag was to pass to fine liners and motorships, and who are going strong today.

The two young steamship clerks who had decided to strike out for themselves were feeling their way, those days. They bought some ships and they chartered some others, starting out in 1859; a quarter of a century later they bought out Patrick Henderson's old, established Albion Shipping Company and tacked "Albion" onto their own names.[1]

At first they picked few "flash packets" for their emigrant trade to New Zealand, so *Euterpe* fitted in nicely; at that, she probably was the slowest one in their fleet. And her addition to the Shaw, Savill ships turned up another of those odd little coincidences, which had to do with her future name: Shaw, Savill had a ship named *Star of India*. She was a lovely old thing, built as late as 1861 but carrying, of all things, quarter galleries, like an eighteenth century frigate.

Euterpe's new life started two days before Christmas, 1871, when she left London under command of a man destined to be anything but a "one tripper." Captain Thomas E. Phillips must have understood her well, for he was to have

---

[1]Brett, *op. cit.*

28

her for the next ten voyages, and each of them was a voyage around the world — from England down and eastward via the Cape of Good Hope, and home across the Pacific's high southern latitudes, past Cape Horn and up the Atlantic. Her first voyage was to Melbourne; after that her destination almost invariably was somewhere in New Zealand. She was back in London October 21, 1872, and cleared for Dunedin December 4; it was going to be sixteen months before she came home. On this, her first New Zealand passage, she reached Dunedin April 14, 1873; it had taken her 117 days to get there.

For weeks Captain Phillips fretted and fumed, waiting for cargoes that were not there. Then he took her over to Newcastle, N. S. W., no doubt with coal in mind, but that was a vain hope, also. In desperation they left Newcastle on July 1 for San Francisco — in ballast; *Euterpe's* people were hoping for better luck on the other side of the Pacific.

They sailed around the south end of New Zealand and crossed the 180th meridian July 19; there was easterly wind to 27° S, 122° W., and the Southeasterly Trades were light. They crossed the Equator August 4 in 120° W and, for a welcome change, picked up southerly winds to 15° N. The Northeasterly Trades also proved light, and they went back out to 141° looking for wind, with no better luck than they had looking for cargo in Newcastle; what wind they found was dead ahead. Finally, on September 24 they towed in through the Golden Gate, 85 days out. In San Francisco she was consigned to Dickerson, Wolf & Co., who seem to have had better luck in rounding up a cargo, and on October 11 she left for that classical destination, "Queenstown, for orders." The orders were to proceed to London, where she arrived April 10, 1874. Cargo was discharged and they sent her around to Liverpool, where she cleared March 25 for Wellington.

Now were to follow six apparently routine voyages of 1875 through 1881 — slow passages had become, unfortunately, routine — which took her up to October 9, 1882. On that day Captain Phillips took her out for the last time, Wellington-bound, on what was to prove to be another 16-month jaunt, again with a San Francisco interlude by way of variety. After discharge she sailed on to Newcastle, where she picked up a cargo of coal for her old San Francisco brokers, and on April 27, 1883, she was under sail. Except for a two-day gale, the passage was marked by too little wind instead of too much. Not until they were above the latitude of San Francisco did they encounter a fine, fair wind and plenty of it, and by that time it was too late. When she picked up her pilot on August 8 they were not 85 days out as on the 1873 passage, but a dismal 102. To add insult to injury, two other British ships arrived from Newcastle the same day; *Melpomene,* which had done it in 84 days, and *Roslyn Castle,* a smaller and older ship which had taken only 81 days to get there.[2] Glumly Captain Phillips got rid of his coal, finally rounded up cargo for Liverpool and bade his second farewell to "the good, gray city" by the Golden Gate.

Her next voyage was from Glasgow, and they cleared April 9, 1884, with passengers and cargo for Otago — with *Euterpe* apparently in one of her more kittenish moods. Towing out behind the *Flying Hurricane,* she started looking for trouble and found it, in the shape of the hapless steamer *Canadian* which, at the moment, was having problems of her own. Specifically, she was stuck in the mud and unable to flee when the hoydenish *Euterpe* took a sudden sheer, refused to answer the helm, and plowed into her stern. In doing so *Euterpe* lost her bowsprit, dropped her figurehead, and carried away most of her head-rigging. They towed her back to Yorkhill Dock for repairs, which took her ten days,

---

[2]*Daily Alta California* (San Francisco) Aug. 8, 1883.

November 14, 1863, was a big day at Ramsey, as they prepared to launch *Euterpe* with appropriate pomp and fanfare.—MANX MUSEUM AND NATIONAL TRUST, RAMSEY, I.O.M.

An on-the-spot painting by J. Burkhill, lithographed by J. Needham, shows a quaint Ramsey Bay as it was in 1859.—MANX MUSEUM AND NATIONAL TRUST, RAMSEY, I.O.M.

Schooners, cutters and sloops below Ramsey's quay wall, with sturdy old buildings rising toward a backdrop of hills.—S. F. MARITIME MUSEUM ASSOCIATION

A familiar sight to *Euterpe* and her people: the picturesque harbor of Port Chalmers, Otago, as it appeared in 1868.—ALEXANDER TURNBULL LIBRARY, WELLINGTON, N. Z.

LOG of the Ship "Euterpe" from Glasgow to Otago

HOUR.	K.	F.	COURSES.	WINDS.	Lee Way.	Barometer.	REMARKS.
1	9		S ¾ S			30.55	Wednesday 2nd July 84
2	10		"	S. W.			
3	10		"				Commences with a brisk but incr-
4	10		"			30.55	easing to Strong breeze with
5	10		"				all sail set.
6	11		.				4 Pm Strong steady breeze with
7	11		"				slight hazy weather, furled
8	11		"			30.50	Miz & fore Royals.
9	11		"	S. W.			
10	11		"				Midnight
11	11		"				Strong steady breeze with
12	11		"			30.48	passing Misty showers
1	11		"				
2	11		"				Strong breeze continues
3	11		"				throughout from S.W.
4	11		"			30.27	6 All sail set.
5	11		"				Carpenter block repairing etc
6	11		"				Crew overhauling buff tackle
7	10		"				blocks, repairing 2 Main topsyl
8	10		"			30.45	
9	10		S ¾	S. W.			11 am Passed a very large
10	10		"				ice berg to the Nord of us
11	10		.				Noon Strong steady breeze.
12	10		"			30.43	Dist. per Log. 152 Miles, S.E. Easterly current 34 in the 24 hours

Course.	Dist.	Dif. Lat.	Dep.	Lat. by Acct.	Lat. by Ob.	Dif. Lon.	Lon. by Acct.	Lon. by Ob.
S ¾ ¾	286 Miles			44.19 South	74 Days out	56.5 ¾		

ON THE LOOK OUT.		NAMES.	LANTERN HUNG OUT.	
From	to	Nelson	From	to
...	...	Reid	...	...
...	...	Kirk	...	...
...	...	Menzies	...	...
...	...	Chadwick	...	...
...	...	Cotter	...	...
...	...	&c. &. O'Doyle Mate	William Paterson Mate	

D. McGREGOR & CO. Official, Nautical and Stationery Warehouses, 44 and 45 Clyde Place, Glasgow ; 32 Cathcart St., Greenock ; and 72 So. Castle St., Liverpool.

Logging a steady 10 knots with everything set, she swept majestically past an iceberg on this, the best day's work in her long history; the date was July 2, 1884, and she logged 286 miles.

HOUR.	K.	F.	COURSES.	WINDS.	Lee Way.	Barometer.	*REMARKS.
1	2		N E ½ N			29.90	Sunday 21st Dec 84
2	2			East			Begins with light baffling
3	2		"	to		29.95	airs then Calm
4	1		"	S E			
5			Calm				
6							Calm; Calm;
7							
8						29 97	
9	1		E ½ N				9.30 A very very light air came
10	1	5		N W			away from the N.W.
11	1	5	"				
12	1	5	"			30. 0	Weather clear sea smooth,
1	2		"				am
2	1		"				
3	1		"				Light air from the N W
4	1		"			30. 7	continues
5	2		"				
6	2		"				Light airs & sea smooth
7	1		"	N.W.		30. 7	as glass
8	1		"				
9	1						
10	2		East				
11	2		"				
12	2					30. 10	Dist. per Log,

Course.	Dist.	Dif. Lat.	Dep.	Lat. by Acct.	Lat. by Ob.	Dif. Lon	Lon. by Acct.	Lon. by Ob.
E S ¼ S	28 Miles				Lat 46. 11 S			Long 135. 59 W

	ON THE LOOK-OUT.		NAMES.		LANTERN HUNG OUT.	
From	8	to 12	Kirk Menzies		From	to
...	...	...			...	...
...	12	4	Orbell Baird		...	...
...	...	...			...	...
...	...	...			...	...
...	...	...			...	...
...	...	...	Geo. L. Hoyle Master.	William Paterson Mate	...	...

D. M'GREGOR & CO., Optical, Nautical, and Stationery Warehouses, 44 and 45 Clyde Place, Glasgow ; 32 Cathcart St., Greenock; and 72 So. Castle St., Liverpool.

Homeward bound, she missed the ". . . strong breeze with all sail set" which had given her that record run of 286 miles a few months before. The frustrating entry, "Calm; Calm; . . ." tells the story.

Her best-known portrait; the year is 1874, and *Euterpe*, yards squared to perfection, lies at the wharf in Port Chalmers, N. Z.—ALEXANDER TURNBULL LIBRARY, WELLINGTON, N. Z.

Rust-streaked from a long voyage, *Euterpe* uses her "cockbilled" yards as cargo booms, to unload at an unidentified wharf.—NAUTICAL PHOTO AGENCY, BECCLES, SUFFOLK

Her new life begins; reduced to bark rig, *Euterpe* seen from under the jibboom of lofty *Centennial*, at San Francisco in 1902.—S. F. MARITIME MUSEUM ASSOCIATION

Securely moored and with upper yards sent down, *Star of India* lies off Nushagak
awaiting the salmon pack, about 1910.—S. F. MARITIME MUSEUM ASSOCIATION

There was an earlier *Star of India*, too—this handsome, Dundee-built ship of 1861,
with quarter-galleries and high poop.—NAUTICAL PHOTO AGENCY, BECCLES, SUFFOLK

From **San Francisco** towards **Bristol Bay**

	H.	K.	¼K.	COURSES	WINDS	LEEWAY	TEMP. AIR	TEMP. WATER	BAROM.	REMARKS 6 day of May 1906
A.M.	1									
	2									
	3									
	4									
	5									
	6									
	7									
	8									
	9									
	10									
	11									
	12									
P.M.	1									
	2									
	3									
	4									
	5									
	6									
	7									
	8									
	9									
	10									
	11								30.08	
	12									

Course	Distance	Diff. of Lat.	Departure	Lat. by D.R.	Lat. by Ob.	Variation	Diff. of Lon.	Lon. in.	Lon. by Ob.
N.b.W.	120	65'	151.1	48°13'		20 E	3 30 W.	160 30	

	H.	K.	½K.	COURSES	WINDS	LEEWAY	TEMP. AIR	TEMP. WATER	BAROM.	REMARKS 7 day of May 1906
A.M.	1					Points				
	2									
	3									
	4					1.				
	5									
	6									
	7									
	8					"				
	9									
	10									
	11									
	12					"				
P.M.	1								30.30	
	2									
	3									
	4					"				
	5									
	6									
	7									
	8					"				
	9									
	10									
	11									
	12					"			30.40	

Course	Distance	Diff. of Lat.	Departure	Lat. by D.R.	Lat. by Ob.	Variation	Diff. of Lon.	Lon. in.	Lon. by Ob.
					49°28'				

On her last voyage as *Euterpe*, we find "Vessel actin Bad. Shipping heavy Water at times"—but there is a later note of cheer: "Aur sick Folks improving." The date is May 6, 1906.

and started again on April 19 — this time, prudently, with two tugs, *Flying Owl* and *Flying Spur*. The next mishap was June 2 when the steward slipped and fell, severely injuring himself. Meanwhile a passenger had complained of the theft of his purse — which the third mate recovered, with the thief, soon after. And also, during what must have been a trying period of readjustment, the second mate had been sent to his cabin in disgrace, for being drunk.

Just after the tug had swung around for home and it was too late to do anything about it, three stowaways had been found on board. So they put them to work and on June 26 one of the trio, John Campbell, was engaged in overhauling topgallant buntlines (which may or may not have needed it) when he lost his hold and fell to the deck nearly a hundred feet below. Although he lingered on for three days, mercifully he never regained consciousness, and they had the first of two funerals for that voyage.

July gales in the Roaring Forties blew several sails out of their boltropes and at one time the beleaguered crew, with spare canvas at a premium, set a tarpaulin in the mizzen rigging to hold her head up to the wind. They saw icebergs (fortunately it was daylight when they encountered them) and there were times when mountainous seas crashed aboard, filling her decks and leaking down below. On July 24 she was pooped by a tremendous sea which flattened her poop railings, flooded out the cabins and smashed in the galley door. The next day Francis Orr, a cabin passenger, died and they had their second funeral. On August 30 they were on soundings, and sighted Nugget Point. Hours later, the wind built up to hurricane force and carried away the truss of the fore lower topsail, but crippled as she was, she came to an anchor the following day. The only cheering note of this Jonah voyage (one of the worst in her career) was the fact that she turned in probably the best day's work she ever made: On July 2 she logged 286 nautical miles, for an average of a shade under 12 knots for the 24 hours. Of course, it was too good to last.

They shifted her over to Napier to load for London, and on December 2 she was underway. December passed, and January, and half of February — and there were unmistakable signs that they should have brought along more food. On February 18 they spoke the bark *Ameer,* of Pictou, on a passage from Cardiff to Batavia; *Ameer* supplied them with bread and sugar. On April 11 they reached London. It had taken them more than four months to do it.

Now that she was in the emigrant trade, that long 'tweendeck, with its row of ports and its somewhat theoretical ventilation, came into its own. The more affluent passengers, of course, occupied those walnut-trimmed cabins under the poop; for those less fortunate it was definitely austere. Despite the prediction at the time of her launching she never sailed as a trooper, but life in her could scarcely have been more grim if she had.

Although the bulkheads in the 'tweendeck were only flimsy curtains, we may rest assured that the ruggedness of the passage was fully equalled by the rigors of propriety. Single women had their dismal bunks at the after end, while the single men were similarly accommodated away up forward. In between was what might be termed a "Buffer State" of married couples with their beds and their belongings and their nosey moppets. When darkness fell, there would be no hanky-panky in the pious ship *Euterpe!*

True Victorian decorum was observed, and there is little doubt that wind and weather permitting, each Sunday passed with appropriate religious services aboard. Perhaps it would be well, therefore, to draw a discreet curtain over a cuisine which today would be regarded with horror by the steward's department of a tramp collier. Mrs. Lillian Barry, who was a passenger in 1874, wrote of the voyage as follows:

"I came out from England to New Zealand in the *Euterpe* as a child with my parents . . . I have heard my parents say how closely they were crowded, the married people and small children all in together and the only privacy being a small curtain in front of their bunks. The single girls were in a part of the vessel called the poop [actually the after 'tween-decks] and they were all gathered together after the evening meal and were not allowed on deck again until the next morning. The food at times was very bad and once when a complaint was made regarding the soup, an investigation revealed a man's sock in the stock pot."[3]

Even more grim was the report of E. F. Owens, a passenger on her longest voyage — nearly five months — to New Zealand. That was in 1879, and to quote from a letter by Owens:

"Food became very short, and all who might recall the early days will remember its lack of variety. As a boy, I can well remember the excitement among the passengers when a rat pie was brought from the galley, and the crowd that followed it from the cook house to the fore part of the ship where the single men bunked."[4]

Aside from having a man washed off the jibboom while furling a jib (he was never seen again) and a death or two from natural causes, her next few years were more or less routine. Scores of other vessels, no doubt, had the same kind of entries as were in *Euterpe's* logs: "Vessel rolling and labouring in a frightful manner" — "Sea mountains high, vessel rolling and straining fearfully" — "Heard noises in after hold, believed to be cargo shifting, but dared not take off hatches"

---

[3]Huycke, Harold: "Colonial Trader to Museum Ship: The Bark *Star of India*"; in *The American Neptune*, April 1950
[4]*Ibid.*

— "Rolling and straining in a most distressing manner, shipping great quantities of water fore and aft." With that flat sheer and little rise to fo'c'sle or poop, our Iron Lady plowed on through the years and through the rolling, tumbling seas of the Atlantic, the Indian and the Pacific Oceans. On her 1887 voyage from London to Melbourne, she encountered a terrific North Atlantic storm on November 19-20; with her fo'c'sle head buried continually and the whole forward deck awash, she began blowing out sails and parting stays. Finally the spanker sheets carried away; the heavy wooden boom flailed drunkenly from side to side, broke the mizzen royal backstay and in so doing broke itself. Then the jagged end of the boom, a huge and lethal lance, charged aft and crashed through the wheel, just missing the helmsman. Luckily, enough spokes were left so that they could control her, and they kept her on the wind.

Considering her penchant for getting into trouble, it is rather surprising that she survived the hazardous cargo which, her logs show, she frequently carried. "At Powder Buoy" — "On Powder Ground — Discharged 1233 packages powder" — such is her record. In those days, it seems to have been perfectly permissible to carry passengers and explosives in the same ship.

The 1888 voyage was unique in that it took her to South America. She got out to Wellington in February of 1889, discharged powder and flax, and loaded hides, wool, tallow and coal; the latter she took to Port Pirie, which she cleared July 10 for Iquique. There she loaded nitrates, and was back in Falmouth March 9, 1890. The next day she was ordered to take her cargo to Hamburg where, after a stay of more than two months, she cleared for Melbourne. A split heel of one of the topmasts sent her back, and she got away, finally, on June 4. It took her until September 15 to make Melbourne, and that night ten Swedish sailors, apparently signed on at Hamburg, went over the side. One of her English sailors followed, although not voluntarily; he was "given in charge" when the mate caught him with seven bottles of schnapps, from a broken case in the cargo. The fact that the customs seal on the hatch had been broken, to give access to the bottled goodies, didn't help him any, and the judge gave him three months. They didn't fool around, in those days.

You will be happy to know that, while lying at Melbourne, they finally got around to shipping a new wheel, to replace the one which had been smashed up and patched up three years before. Then they went around to Napier, to load for home.

The classical tale of the master who entered in the log "This day the Mate was drunk," to which the mate retaliated a few days later with "This day the Captain was sober" may not have happened in *Euterpe*, although at least one case involving a rift in the high command did get into her log on the homeward voyage from Napier to London in 1891. It seems that the chief officer was a stickler for protocol as he saw it, and took a dim view of having the second mate bring him directives from the master. It wound up with this terse entry: "H. Willis Jones, chief officer, ordered to remain in his cabin owing to refusal to obey orders of Capt. Thos. Bowling, through the second mate."

An intriguing novelty in log entries showed up on the very next outward voyage, and might well be described as "The Mystery of the Elusive Aroma." Although of no serious consequence, it was followed by events which proved a bit unpleasant. It all started out when it was noted in the log on October 21, 1892, that a powerful smell of whiskey was coming up the vent, out of the hold. About then other things occurred to occupy their time, such as the big sea which slapped against the rudder, knocked the helmsman away from the wheel — that nice, new wheel — and broke off all of the spokes, close up to the nave. They did some fancy balancing with her sails, the carpenter worked all night, and by dawn they had a crude new wheel and were back on their course. The smell of whiskey continued, and on November 21, as was the weekly custom (when she wasn't completely under water) they opened up the main hatch to ventilate. It's a good thing they did; the coal in her cargo was up to 90° and steaming badly, and the entire main hold was drenched with sweat. They hove 10 tons of coal up into the 'tween-decks to let it cool, which it finally started to do a fortnight later. They had trouble steering, they sighted an iceberg uncomfortably close, and finally just before Christmas, they got in at Port Chalmers. Meanwhile, the tantalizing odor of whiskey which they could not reach continued to come up out of the hold. Early in January they got to that part of the cargo, and found that the shifting of other merchandise had clobbered two casks of Scotch.

They went down to Dunedin, loaded wool and headed for home. Two weeks out, a mysterious hole appeared in the forward hatch tarpaulin; it developed that rats had eaten their way up and out of the hold, through the canvas. In one day, shortly afterward, they trapped 32 rats, plus an undisclosed number dispatched by the ship's cat and ship's dog. Then the rats got back at them by eating their way out through the canvas jacket which goes around the mainmast, where it comes through the deck. It is just as well that, by now, *Euterpe* had quit hauling emigrants, and was a mere freighter.

Hardly had she stuck her nose out of Liverpool on her 1894 voyage to Dunedin when she ran into a gale of king-size proportions. Discretion proving the better part of valor, she put in at Belfast until the weather became better, and then continued on Down Under. But such things were all in the day's work for deepwater ships, and she continued shoving that tough iron hull through fair weather and foul, on her passages around the world.

Part 2 New Trades, New Flags

THE CASE OF THE DUBIOUS HAWAIIAN

NOW HER DAYS AS A BRITISH SHIP WERE DRAWING TO A CLOSE. Three more voyages took up her time until October 4, 1897, when she left East India Dock for Greenock, to top off with powder. When she dropped her pilot off the Hook of Waterford on December 3, she was bidding her final farewell to the British Isles.

On her way out she playfully tossed her people about, and a few things let go here and there, but she got to Port Chalmers safely and discharged her cargo. Then her fo'c'sle hands proceeded to relax in a big way, and, to a certain extent, so did the afterguard. It was duly logged that the second mate was sent to his stateroom for being drunk; that night he went AWOL, came back to spend the next day recuperating in his bunk, and quietly slipped ashore the same evening. This time, when he came back and tottered up the gangway, he was promptly and properly sacked.

From Port Chalmers she went over to Newcastle to take on coal for Honolulu, and she sailed on April 20, 1898. It was a significant destination, and hints that Shaw, Savill already had sold their faithful but kittenish old servant to J. J. Moore of San Francisco. Whether her people knew or not, *Euterpe* seems to have known that something was in the wind, and she resented it. She retaliated with a slow leak — to say nothing of getting her mizzen hatch stove in and a lot of water below, and carrying away her fore lower topsail yard again. In approaching Diamond Head on the afternoon of July 31, she grounded, but did not hurt herself, and went on to a Honolulu wharf.

On the passage up from Newcastle it seems that she had, more or less, become a Hawaiian vessel. On July 2, John J. Moore reported that he had sold *Euterpe, Star of Italy,* and *Star of France* to Lincoln Spencer, and on the same day Spencer received a "temporary" Hawaiian register from the Hawaiian Consul at Seattle. On August 3, Spencer, stating that he was a native-born Hawaiian citizen, went to get a permanent Hawaiian register for *Star of Italy* — and was turned down on the grounds that the Joint Resolution of Annexation to the United States ended Hawaii's right to register vessels. Spencer went to law about it, and on November 4 the Supreme Court of Hawaii, holding that registration was a municipal matter and hence not affected by the annexation law, ordered the Collector General of Customs to give Spencer his registration. He finally got it for *Star of Italy* on November 11.[1]

By way of explanation, the impending annexation of Hawaii had paved the way for some interesting additions to the American merchant marine. Under existing law, American registry is denied to foreign-built vessels, unless they have been so badly damaged that their repair, in an American yard, comes to 40 percent of their original cost. However, if the United States were to acquire another nation in toto, obviously that nation's ships could come along, too. And this was happening just as the wooden-built American "medium clippers" were wearing out. In most services, sailing ships had had their day, with two possible exceptions: the export timber trade, and the Alaska fisheries. Aware of this, Moore and other San Francisco shipping men had been picking up some perfectly lovely, British-built ships and barks, and putting them under Hawaiian registry. In addition to those

---

[1] Public Archives, State of Hawaii, Honolulu.

named, the list included *Star of Bengal, Star of Russia, Willscott* and a superb four-masted bark called *Falls of Clyde*.[2]

Meanwhile, both international events and the unloading of *Euterpe* had been going on apace. The new second mate was almost done in by a mutinous sailor, and another of her hands was collared by the local constabulary as he attempted to defect to a schooner in which life appeared to be, and no doubt was, a bit more serene. President McKinley had signed the Treaty of Annexation on July 7, and on August 12 the Stars and Stripes were raised over the Executive Building of the former Hawaiian government, amid appropriate speech-making and whatever. Of all of the Hawaiian-American hocus-pocus, this was the only thing to get into *Euterpe's* log:

"Friday, August 12th, 1898. A. M. — Morning Came up Showery. 7, began working coals. P. M. — Broke the crank of the Engine finished the day having Discharged 97. tons . . . "Hawaiian Islands" Inexed [sic] by "America" today General Holiday on shore."

Still with nothing more to go on than a temporary or provisional register granted *in absentia* by the consul of a nation whose days were numbered, *Euterpe* wound up her Honolulu business; after prudently stowing her fore and main royal yards below, she towed out on September 6, in ballast, bound for Royal Roads, B. C. She made it in 23 days and then shifted over to Quartermaster Harbor, for a grueling period of scrubby-rubby which could mean but one thing — drydocking and survey. They got the dunnage boards up into the 'tweendecks and unloaded all but some 300 tons of ballast, which was trimmed to amidships. She was drydocked and painted, the surveyors surveyed the part that was clear of ballast; they trimmed the ballast back again, and started getting the anchor chains up on deck for examination.

---

[2]*Ibid.*

By now, the crew was fit to be tied. Small wonder that, on October 21, it was noted in the log that "When looking around this morning . . . found all the Hauling lines cut in several places . . . all cut maliciously . . ." Just the same, the work went on until the morning of October 29 when Captain H. Longmuir, last of her British masters, herded his men ashore. The log entry for that day is historically significant: "Crew all got paid off before British Consul at 10 a.m." That was, in reality, the end of the British ship *Euterpe*.

Already the lumber was going into her for her entry into the export timber trade, where those two square ports, cut into her stern, were to be important; they are, of course, for handling stuff too long to go down the hatches. Whether owned by J. J. Moore, or the Pacific Colonial Shipping Company, or Lincoln Spencer, she completed loading and left Tacoma for Port Adelaide, Australia, on November 20, 1898. A winter gale kept her decks almost continuously flooded; three days out, an extra big one came aboard, flooding out the cabin. A bulkhead between the cabin and a storeroom carried away and her new master, Captain C. G. Saxe, was caught under the avalanche of stores and badly injured. For reasons which are not noted in her log, she put in at Honolulu December 29, having been 39 hectic days at sea. Obviously, she went in to see how her citizenship was coming along — and what a day she chose to do so! It was the very day that Spencer, having been denied permanent Hawaiian registry for *Euterpe*, was going to the Supreme Court about it, along with the frustrated owners of *Willscott* and *Falls of Clyde*.[3] Sorrowfully, no doubt, *Euterpe* towed to sea on

[3]It took the Supreme Court until June 5, 1899, a matter of nearly six months, to rule that the Collector General had to issue them Hawaiian registers, whether he liked it or not. The owner of *Star of Russia* and *Star of France*, through his attorney had threatened to hold the Collector General responsible for loss of trade and had asked for an extension of the "temporary registry," which had been denied (Public Archives).

40

the last day of 1898, and turned her long jibboom once more in the general direction of Port Adelaide, where she arrived March 6, 1899.

She discharged her timber, was gale-bound (that wretched fore topsail crane carried away again, this time right in port) and finally went around to Newcastle to discharge copper ore and flour, picking up Honolulu-bound coal for the return voyage. Back in Honolulu July 15, she discharged her coal but seems to have left the matter of her registry strictly alone — perhaps because in February the United States Attorney General had ruled that Hawaii could no longer register vessels. The discharge of coal had to be halted at one time because she became alarmingly cranky, but they sent out for some more ballast and finished the job. She then went on to Port Townsend and Seattle, arriving September 1, a still somewhat dubious Hawaiian citizen. They towed her over to Port Ludlow to load lumber, and on October 31 took departure from Cape Flattery, bound for Fremantle.

For *Euterpe* and her people, the Nineteenth Century ended inauspiciously. Her deckload of lumber started to get adrift during a year-end storm, but they got it secured again, and she made Fremantle, 148 days out, as March was ending. On May 10 she left for Newcastle where again her scanty stability was noted in the log on June 28; they had to halt the discharge of ballast ". . . as vessel nearly on her beam ends." The next day, as she swung with the tide, her stern tangled up with the bowsprit of the barkentine *Sir John Franklin*. She lost two stanchions and 15 feet of railing; damage to the barkentine was tactfully ignored in her report.

Full of coal, she got away from Newcastle on July 10 for Kahului, T. H., where she arrived September 16. Trying to head toward the pilotboat she ran aground off Spreckelsville, and two tugs were unable to get her off.

Her captain chartered the steamer *Mokului* to take the chief mate to Honolulu to get help. Luckily, the *Mokului* loaned them a spare anchor, which was dropped astern. As the wind rose and she started to pound, this anchor was all that kept her from going hopelessly further up onto the reef. The weather got bad the next day and she parted both this line and another which they had carried out astern. Heaven knows what would have become of her had not the famous old tug *Fearless* appeared about then, with *Euterpe's* mate aboard. They got 100 tons of coal overboard to lighten her and *Fearless* snaked her back into deep water. But in doing so the rudder hit the reef, was driven eight inches up through her deck, and did not reseat. Also, she now had a slow leak of about an inch an hour. They towed her to Honolulu for discharge and repairs.

Historically, the stranding at Spreckelsville was far less important than certain paper work which went on meanwhile at the Honolulu Customhouse — by this time, American rather than Hawaiian. There on October 30, 1900, the provisional register issued by the Hawaiian Consul at Seattle was surrendered and she got what appears to have been her first American document; it was Temporary Enrollment No. 44 and lists the Pacific Colonial Shipping Company, a California corporation, as her owners.[4] She now was the American ship *Euterpe.* Back of it was quite a bit of legal maneuvering.

On August 17, 1899, the Attorney General of the Republic of Hawaii had given an opinion that the provisional registers were not recognized, that the ships were British-built and ownership by Hawaiian citizens was not genuine, but only for the purpose of getting Hawaiian registry for foreigners. On September 18 President McKinley (who no doubt was being needled by American shipbuilders, unions and do-

---

[4]U. S. Customs Records, Honolulu

gooders) forbade any further registering of Hawaiian vessels. So, for a couple of years, *Euterpe* had been sailing up and down the Pacific with a document which apparently was of little value.

Luckily for these ships, the Hawaiian Organic Act, which became a law on June 14, 1900, had a section which provided that any Hawaiian-registered vessel as of August 12, 1898, owned by United States citizens, ". . . together with the following named vessels claiming Hawaiian register, Star of France, Euterpe, Star of Russia, Falls of Clyde, and Willscott . . ." were entitled to full American registry.[5]. Congress had made a decent woman of *Euterpe*.

Now supposedly as fit as a fiddle, she was towed to Kaanapali, where she loaded 27,000 bags of sugar and on November 23 was underway for San Francisco. Two days later they found that she was leaking again — about 22 buckets a day — but they kept on, and on December 19 were off San Francisco. The bar was breaking and there was no tug in sight, so they hove to. The next day the captain said the hell with it; he squared her yards and plunged on, across the seething bar, without tug or pilot. They anchored, then proceeded under tow to Oakland, to discharge.

She spent the first week of 1901 in Hunter's Point Drydock for a survey, as Pacific Colonial now had found a buyer for her, and there is a log notation dated January 16, 1901: "Vessel now sold to Alaska Packers Assoc." She was on her way to becoming *Star of India*, but it was going to take some six years to do it.

Already, however, she had started loading lumber for Melbourne, so she was not to enter the Alaska salmon trade at once. She left San Francisco February 10 on a voyage marked by nothing more serious than the blowing out her mains'l and shipping a sea that carried away a poop ladder,

[5]Sec. 98, 48 U. S. C. A. 509.

43

flooded out the fo'c'sle and smashed the binnacle of the standard compass. She got to Melbourne, went on to Newcastle to load coal and was back in San Francisco late in the summer of 1901.

That winter she went into a shipyard, for some rather fantastic changes. After being chipped inside and out (the Alaska Packers believed in plain but well kept ships) they laid a new main deck and new 'tweendeck. The forward house was rebuilt, and a Murray Brothers' donkey engine, boiler, steam pump and condenser were installed. There is evidence that, until then, she had carried an old-fashioned log windlass, probably the one now on display in the San Francisco Maritime Museum. It was replaced by a Providence capstan windlass, which could be turned by a messenger chain running back to the donkey engine. The poop was stripped off, and extended almost to the mainmast in order to provide quarters for fishermen and cannery hands; this increased her gross tonnage to 1318. Alterations were made in the after cabins, and a Chinese galley was installed below. Water tanks for an additional 5400 gallons went into her hold, and a 1200-gallon tank was placed in the donkey room.

Riggers, meanwhile, were not idle. Out came the old mizzenmast with its yards, to be replaced with a wooden mast and topmast, rigged with boom and spanker gaff; *Euterpe* now was a bark, rather than a ship.

For the benefit of those to whom life without garlic and chilies is out of the question, a Mexican galley was installed under her fo'c'sle head. Bunks for the cooks and baker went into the forward end of the deckhouse. The poop extension took care of some 54 fishermen and cannery hands, while the after end of the 'tweendecks, with tiers of bunks three high down the center and two high on the sides, accommodated 63 more. The rest — and at times she carried more than 200 all told — were quartered forward.

By the spring of 1902 she was ready for her score of annual passages between San Francisco and the canneries of Bristol Bay. The smart "port painted" hull of the Shaw, Savill ships had succumbed to the grimly functional black of the Alaska Packers. Her spars were a dismal shade of French yellow; the same color, trimmed with "boxcar red," was slapped onto bulwarks, deckhouse, and even her teak skylight. For several years she retained her gaff-headed spanker, but finally it too, fell before the advance of functional efficiency — and smaller crews. It eventually was replaced by that hallmark of the West Coast sailing vessel, the leg-o-mutton spanker, and the gaff topsail was superseded by a ringtail.

If the Lord Bishop — and Mr. Callister — could have seen her now!

DOWN TO HER MARKS WITH SALMON

AT 7 A.M. MARCH 18, 1902, YOU MIGHT SAY, *Euterpe's* LIFE as an Alaska Packer began; that was when the tug got her in tow, bound for sea and for the icy waters of the Far North. Although Captain George Swanson's crew was small, so far as sailors went, she was well packed with humanity. There were fishermen and cannery workers, with heavy emphasis on Italians and Chinese, and they were going to be gone until early fall, when Alaska would begin to freeze up.

Off the heads, at noon, she let go the towline and made sail on what was supposed to be a simple voyage to Prince William Sound. That night the wind freshened and they took in sail, and *Euterpe*, who no doubt keenly felt her descent in the social scale from passenger carrier to the fisheries, pulled a brand new one out of her bag of tricks:

"7 a.m. on March 19th found fore lowermast had settled down about 4 inches slacking up all fore rigging . . . Started to secure foremast by swiftening rigging to geather fisher men all refused to work if not returning to port . . . all hands said ship was to deep loaded So the captain come to the conclusion to put back." And within hours she was back off the Farallones, those picturesque if dismal islets some 25 miles off San Francisco, signalling for a tug.

In the same hand and in more or less conventional spelling, the log goes on, in port, until March 22; then, quite obviously, someone else took over the keeping of her journal, and a perusal of the log becomes a real chore. Gone with the

Log of the *Star of Juda* from *San Francisco* towards *Bristol Bay*

H.	K.	F.	COURSES	WINDS, &c.	LEE-WAY	DEVIA-TION	REMARKS *April 18 1918*
1							
2							
3			-				1ºº Calm & light SE'y winds
4	16		West	S E		1'E	weather overcast cta smooth
5							
6							
7							8ºº No change.
8	14		W	S.E		1E	At 9⁴⁵ All one Picardo Ramirez Mexican
9							Cannery worker tried to comit suicide
10							by cutting his throat with a razor,
11							he was ate once taken aft his wound
							tied up and dressed and given all
							Possible care
12	6		W	Calm			H. Marzan Master C. J. Carlson Mate

Dist. by Log	Course and Distance		Latitude	Longitude	Barometer	Thermometer	Inches in the Well	Bearing and Distance
77 Miles	Acc.	N63W 86 M			a. m.	a. m.	a. m.	
	Obs.	- --	36 55N	140 10W	Noon	Noon	Noon	
					p. m. 8 days out	p. m.	p. m.	

H.	K.	F.	COURSES	WINDS, &c.	LEE-WAY	DEVIA-TION	REMARKS 1
1							
2							
3							
4	6		W	Calm		1E	Calm and light winds Sky overcast
5							long Wly Swell
6							
7							
8	9		WNW	Calm and light		1W	Lights lookout and general routine
9							
10							
11							12ºº Midnight no
12	7		WNW	" "			H. Marzan Master

In 1960, Carl Carlson still remembered the gory details of the attempted suicide of Ricardo Ramirez on the 1918 passage from San Francisco towards Bristol Bay.

Heavy traffic off Unimak Pass; under gray skies, in the spring of 1918, eight of the Packers' ships wait to get through.—S. F. MARITIME MUSEUM ASSOCIATION

A leading wind and a lively sea as *Star of India* heads home through Unimak Pass, at the end of the 1918 season.—LT. COMDR. M. A. RANSOM, U.S.C.G. (RET.)

In those days, the sky was thick with masts and spars as the Alaska Packers' fleet lay in winter quarters at Alameda. The four-masted bark in the center of this 1916 view is *Star of Greenland.*—PHOTO BY AUTHOR

Disaster was close to *Star of India* when her people saw *Abner Coburn* wrecked in Alaska in 1918. The crew (foreground) was saved.—s. f. MARITIME MUSEUM ASSOCIATION

Drifting ice menaces the anchored fleet, off the Nushagak River. The bark at left center probably is *Star of Finland*.—s. f. MARITIME MUSEUM ASSOCIATION

There were times when even *Star of India's* old friend and frequent rescuer, the steamer *Nushagak*, was hopelessly stuck in the ice.—S. F. MARITIME MUSEUM ASSOCIATION

Sturdy salmon-fishing boats line the beach under the windows of the bleak cannery buildings at Nushagak.—S. F. MARITIME MUSEUM ASSOCIATION

With lots of salmon to catch and not too long a season, *Star of India's* fishermen lost no time in getting their boats under sail.—CAPTAIN OTTO WEIDEMANN

In the Bering Sea, late summer of 1921; *Star of India* makes sail as she heads for home, with her share of the "pack" aboard.—CAPTAIN OTTO WEIDEMANN

A small but sturdy tug gets the fishermen away when there is no wind—and what's in that jug is nobody's business!—CAPTAIN OTTO WEIDEMANN

A fair wind, but not much of it; looking aft from the end of the jibboom at *Star of India's* frugally platched canvas, about 1917.—CAPTAIN OTTO WEIDEMANN

wind was the Spencerian script of those now forgotten Shaw, Savill mates in their neat blue uniforms, and gone was that at times flowery wording of the text. No longer did she "pitch fearfully" nor did she "labour in a most distressing manner." The written prose of her new people was, at times, like the APA ships themselves, strictly functional and unadorned.

The last windjammers out of San Francisco were officered largely by a robust lot of skippers and mates of Scandinavian origin; many of them had obtained American citizenship by the simple process of going over the side of some hard and hungry Cape Horner, to seek a berth in the better paying — and far better feeding — American ships. In those days, such informal entry was no bar to naturalization. And considering the calibre of the men involved, both the American merchant marine and the nation at large were enriched thereby. These men had been at sea since childhood; they could smell bad weather approaching, they knew when and how to make sail and to take it in, and their grasp of nautical astronomy was good enough to get them there and bring them back. English, however, was not their native tongue. They soon learned to play it by ear, but writing the oddly spelled words was, at times, a real problem. Wherefor, in what can only be called a phonetic spelling with a Scandinavian accent, we get this story of how *Euterpe* got to sea at last:

"April 17 . . . atte 11 A m the Thogg bots harser Was sekurde toving aute at 1 P m Lattigo the harser Sails var satten During the time toving aute at 4 P m farallonse Bare NW Dis of 12 Mils . . . Ankarse sekurde on the foxselhad . . . From san Francisco to Brestol bay . . "[1]

---

[1] Anyone who has been around the West Coast steam schooners can, of course, take this in his stride. To others the following translation may be of assistance: "April 17 . . . At 11 a.m. the tug boat's hawser was secured; towing out. At 1 p.m. let go the hawser. Sails were set during the time towing out. At 4 p.m. Farallones bore NW, Distant 12 miles . . . Anchors secured on the fo'c'sle head . . . From San Francisco toward Bristol Bay."

But let no East Coaster look down his nose at English as written, out of San Francisco, in 1902. They tell the story of a famous master of clipper ships who "wrote" an autobiography full of such literary cream puffs as "Beneath my feet the whole fabric of the ship quivered, a thing alive, as she plunged on through the seething brine." Some small-minded person dug up one of the old man's log books and was charmed to read "at 1 P. m. sandy Huk boar West by No, distent 2 miles, from wich i taken my Departer."

Her foremast tantrum over, *Euterpe* settled down philosophically to her new life. Instead of ammunition, emigrants and general merchandise, she now was down to her marks with coal, tin plate, box shook,[2] oil in which the fish would be packed and coal with which it would be cooked — and a polyglot "passenger list" of fishermen and cannery hands.

Captain Carl J. Carlson, who served aboard her as mate some years later, thus describes her "recruitment" procedure:

"We left San Francisco with about 200 men aboard, half of whom were the so-called cannery gang; the rest were fishermen and beach gang and cooks and so on. It was a motley crew. A Chinaman was the prime contractor for the company and he recruited his wherever he could — Chinese, Japs, Mexicans, Filipinos. The other part of the crew, all hired by the company, were the mechanics, technicians, carpenters, the steward and his department, the ship's officers and about fifty fishermen who also sailed the ship.

"There was a lot of drunkenness and fighting until things settled down. After getting up to Alaska it was hard work and long hours — but then, a good fisherman could make on

---

[2] Instead of shipping space-consuming empty cans, flat tin plate was sent north, and the cans were fabricated in Alaska; the same was true of the wooden boxes, which went north in the form of box shook, nails and labels. With today's universal use of pulpboard cartons, the term "box shook" is about to bid farewell to our language.

the average about $500 for about four months, which was very good in those days. The fishermen who stood watches and sailed the ship were all good sailors and had it easy; three watches and twenty or more men per watch and a wheel turn about twice a week — good old days!"

There seem to have been times, however, when men with square-rigger training were less plentiful; Captain Ole Lee, another of her alumni, recalls that he was one of nine men drafted from other Packers' ships when her master flatly refused to sail her back to San Francisco without at least ". . . one full watch of white men!"

She was vastly different now from the ship she had been in her colonial days. No one bothered to get out a ship's newspaper, nor was hymn singing rampant on Sundays. Back in the officers' quarters a funnel-mouthed Edison phonograph, from time to time ground out scratchy music from a modest "album" of wax cylinder records. Among the Italian or Mexican fishermen and cannery hands, someone would occasionally drag out a guitar or a mandolin, or the men would loll around the deck to smoke and gossip until utter boredom ended conversation.

The chief diversion was gambling, and the fan-tan games which were operated under the aegis of the Orientals aboard, were traditional. And they were serious business indeed, for they started by the time the San Francisco tug dropped them off the Farallones and kept on until another tug was snaking them into the Nushagak River, in far-off Alaska.

At night, those games must have provided material which would have delighted a Dore or a George Bellows, as the players carried on in the murky half light of the 'tween decks. While some of the Packers' ships, in later years, got Delco-powered electric lights and even wireless, *Euterpe* was not fated to be one of them. In the relative luxury of the cabin and the officers' quarters there were kerosene lamps, but her crew

49

space was lit, at night, only by thick paraffin candles mounted in big, square bulkhead lanterns. It was not, however, either penuriousness nor social distinction which led to this scheme for lighting the ship; it was a stark matter of safety. Fights and drinking being not unknown, the very thought of oil lamps in the crowded fishermen's quarters is chilling. So, to the dim yellow glow of candlelight the games went on, amid grotesquely shifting shadows and the mutterings of the players.

Ships engaged in the fisheries tend, at times, to be untidy, and it is unlikely that *Euterpe* smelled much like a rose from the 20 or 30 pigs which occupied an improvised sty atop her main hatch. There also were voyages, it is said, on which a cow or two traveled in her, in addition, of course, to the traditional coop full of chickens. When these things were gone, it became strictly a matter of salt meat and canned goods.

But, while the three sets of cooks toiled and the idlers played fan-tan, there were such things as wheel and lookout duty for her skeleton crew of sailors. The pump well had to be sounded regularly to detect possible leakage, and of course they had to be constantly alert to such matters as the proper brightness of the sidelights. All of this maritime housekeeping was being duly recorded:

"at 3 P m hald Down the messen top mast stay sail and Rift the spanker . . . at 12 P m tock in the far the gallen sail and the mainsail it is Bloing strong . . . Wind enkrising al de time . . . ships dutis atandat tu . . ."[3]

She reached Nushagak May 22 and unloaded men and cargo; for the next three months she would lie at anchor with

---

[3]Trimmed up a bit, this now reads: "At 3 p.m. hauled down the mizzen-topmast stays'l and reefed the spanker . . . at 12 p.m. took in the fore t'gallant sail and the mains'l — it is blowing strong. Wind increasing all the time . . . Ship's duties attended to."

only the master and the cook aboard, while the rest of her people caught the salmon, or had to do with getting it cooked, into cans, boxed and loaded on board. Finally the short season's pack was all under hatches, and on August 22 the log takes up again:

"Bark Euterpe from Nushagak toward San Francisco — at 2 P m borded the harser hove opp the Port ankar an proceded toving aute Being Claude and Rain fore an aft sails var satt at 4 P m satt the sqvar sails at 6:30 lattgo the harser . . ."[4]

Now she was free of the tug, and on her own again, starting the first voyage home from Bristol Bay. On September 10 they picked up the Farallones and a tug came wallowing out through the swells to take them in tow. Sails were clewed up and furled as they towed in through the Golden Gate and went alongside a pier to discharge cargo and pay off the crew. Then — over to Oakland Estuary, to go into winter quarters. It gave them a good chance to get at the ailing heel of her foremast.

The 1903 voyage began from San Francisco April 13 and ended when she returned September 8. It was uneventful, while she was at sea. At anchor in the Nushagak River, however, it was a different story. There was a good deal of ice coming down the river, and although they put the helm first to starboard and then to port, swinging her in the current to dodge the ice cakes, a big one lodged across her bows, and carried away the anchor chain. Fortunately, they let go the other one in time to keep her from going on the beach. Later they picked up the lost anchor, so everyone was happy.

---

[4]"Bark Euterpe, from Nushagak toward San Francisco — at 2 p.m. boarded the [tug's] hawser; hove up the port anchor and proceeded towing out [the weather] being cloudy, and rain. Fore-and-aft sails were set. At 4 p.m. set the square sails. At 6:30 let go the hawser . . ."

Two days after she left San Francisco for Bristol Bay the following spring — it was on April 17, 1904 — one of the "passengers" attempted suicide by jumping overboard. They backed the yards, got a boat over the side and picked him up, but he seems to have Jonahed the voyage. There was minor trouble of one kind and another; on April 28 the log reflects "Ships Dutis atandat tu and a fiu fisierman being Drunke for seviral Days" and on May 6 one of the crew fell on deck and broke a leg. A week later one of the Chinese died, and whether or not his restless spirit had anything to do with it, it took them three days to beat through Unimak Pass. They didn't get to Bristol Bay until June 5; it had taken them 49 days to make it. This, of course gave them a really short season, for they left on August 19, and were back in San Francisco September 11.

Next year they did a little better. They got away on April 14, 1905, and reached Bristol Bay 33 days later, having gone through Unimak Pass during a light snowstorm. The summer was routine, as was the voyage home, at least until they got into San Francisco Bay. They were on soundings September 14 and hove to in a dense fog, but it cleared up and they took their tug off Point Reyes. They anchored briefly off Meiggs Wharf, then got up the hook and headed up the bay with the tug *Sea Fox* providing the power. Off Washington Street Wharf trouble appeared, this time in the form of the little stern-wheeler *Fort Bragg*, and the mate solemnly recorded that a collision occurred "between the side of the steamer Fort Bragg and our bow." Damage appears to have been slight; *Euterpe* went on to unload her cargo and then to head for Oakland Creek to go into winter quarters. It gave them a chance to shift ballast, clean out the limbers and build a gutterway for the bilge water, as she now carried her ballast between the frames, making the limbers — small holes in the frames, near the keel, to allow a flow of bilge

52

water to the pumps — all but useless. They also caulked the seams in her poop deck, and scaled her all around, for three plates up from the waterline.

"A ship," the old saying goes, "is never finished until she's sunk."

CHAPTER VI

A STAR IS BORN

To THE ALASKA PACKERS, THAT SERIO-COMIC GAMBIT OF BRITish ships going through a Honolulu cocoon stage, to emerge flapping the Stars and Stripes, wasn't funny; it was wonderful. It pointed the way for augmenting, and in the end replacing with iron and steel ships the fine old medium clippers which they were using, ships like *Santa Clara, Llewellyn J. Morse, Indiana* and *Bohemia.* These lovely Down Easters were built of wood, and a wooden ship is anything but immortal. Mother Nature's ugly side includes such things as dry rot, and nasty little creatures generically known as "marine borers." What they can do to a ship's planking would amaze you.

The Packers lost no time in taking advantage of this situation. Having bought *Euterpe* they began picking up others, and by 1906 they had eight of them, including four handsome ships which had worn the colors of the famous line of "Corry's Irish Stars" out of Belfast: *Star of France, Star of Bengal, Star of Italy* and *Star of Russia.* Far in the dismal future, fortunately, lay such dreadful "fleet name" appellations as *Esso Baytown, Sinclair Superflame* or — hang onto your hats — *Cities Service Koolmotor.* In the palmy days of the APA, ships still bore ship-like names; the Madison Avenue influence was yet to come. There was a pleasant ring to *Star of Bengal.* Why not start the name of each of the Packers' new ships with the word "Star"?

It was a perfectly logical, perfectly reasonable idea, and it should have been perfectly simple. What kept it from being so was bureaucratic technicalities and congressional suspicion — although the Packers eventually won their point. The initial request for authority to change the names of six ships was duly sent to the Commission of Navigation, of the then Department of Commerce and Labor. The Packers set forth that they would like to rename *Abbey Palmer* (originally the capsized *Blairmore*) as *Star of England,* to address *Balclutha* in the future as *Star of Alaska* and to make *Euterpe, Himalaya* and *Coalinga,* respectively, *Star of India, Star of Peru* and *Star of Chile.* The Bureau of Navigation nodded gravely and looked into the matter only to find that some, if not all of the ships involved were covered by mortgages. This was, forsooth, a serious matter: Was some City Slicker from San Francisco planning to slide out from under a mortgage by changing the name of his ships, and blithely sailing away for an unknown coral atoll? The Commissioner of Navigation would have no part of any such dealings, although in denying the request he graciously conceded that ". . . application may be made to Congress for special legislation waiving the legal objection . . ."[1]

If the Commissioner thought that by suggesting such a normally tedious course he was getting the Alaska Packers out of his hair, he displayed a woeful ignorance of the type of men who sat behind those golden oak desks at No. 111 California Street. Petitioning Congress was exactly what they did, and they did it without delay. On March 30, 1906, Representative Julius Kahn of California introduced a bill captioned HR-17600, directing the Commissioner of Navigation to stir his stumps, and change those names. It hardly created a ripple — until Representative Champ Clark, of Missouri, raised a suspicious eyebrow. He demanded a formal second to the bill "for the sake of information," and then asked an ominous question: *Are these, or are they not, American ships?*

---

[1]Bu. of Nav. Corresp. File No. 40324.

Just what Congress would be doing, running around changing the names of Siamese or Ecuadorean ships, is not clear; it must be remembered, however, that to many an inland congressman, it is traditional to view anything maritime with suspicion if not with outright alarm. Fortunately there are other congressmen from fresh-water areas who do not pursue this course, and one of them, Representative Charles H. Grosvenor of Ohio, rose to *Euterpe's* defense. He assured his colleagues that ". . . these small ships" were indeed American, and that their owners were motivated by nothing more nefarious than a wish to rid themselves of ". . . a lot of almost unpronounceable names." The Gentleman from Missouri was placated, and the House of Representatives passed the bill.[2] It went through the Senate without question or debate, and on June 29, 1906, President Theodore Roosevelt signed it as Public Law 365, 59th Congress. For the second time, *Euterpe* had been up before Congress. There was to be a third time, as *Star of India*, more than half a century later.

When they bought *Euterpe* and thus got into the metal-hulled ship business, the Packers owned thirteen wooden vessels. Eventually, in addition to the transplanted Down Easters which retained their original names, they would have no less than nineteen iron or steel square riggers to send up to Nushagak or Naknek or Kvichak each summer, and to nestle together at the foot of Alameda's Paru Street each winter.[3]

In wooden shipbuilding, America had excelled; with metal hulls, however, it was a less inspiring story. By around 1890, iron had been abandoned in favor of steel, and con-

[2]Congressional Record, June 19, 1906.

[3]Huycke, Harold: "The Great Star Fleet," in *Yachting*, New York, Feb. and Mar. 1960.

currently our big days in the wooden ship business were ending; the last American full-rigged ship, built of wood, was *Aryan,* launched at Phippsburg, Maine, in 1893. In the square-rigger field we built only three ships of iron, *T. F. Oakes, Clarence S. Bement* and *Tillie E. Starbuck* — and nine steel ones. The latter, all launched at Bath, Maine, were *Dirigo, Arthur Sewall, Edward Sewall, Wm. P. Frye, Erskine M. Phelps, Acme, Astral* and *Atlas* (all four-masted barks) and the three-masted bark *Kaiulani.*[4] The Packers eventually got all of the steel ones still in commission. These were the old Standard Oil "Three Big A" case oil ships *Acme, Astral* and *Atlas,* which became *Star of Poland, Star of Zealand* and *Star of Lapland; Edward Sewall,* renamed *Star of Shetland,* and *Kaiulani,* which they called *Star of Finland.*

Some of their other acquisitions obtained American documentation through big repair bills in American yards, after fire or dismasting. Such were the cases of *Star of Scotland,* the former British (and subsequently American) *Kenilworth,* and *Star of Holland,* ex- *Zemindar,* ex- *Otto Gildemeister,* ex-*Homeward Bound.* The former German ship *Steinbek,* seized as a war prize in 1917 and renamed *Northern Light,* was bought by the Packers in 1922 and was renamed *Star of Falkland.*[5]

But let us get back to April 14, 1906, and the things which were happening in California. For one thing, *Euterpe* was towing out through the Golden Gate with 62 whites and 181 Chinese and Japanese cannery hands aboard. Those who had not already got into the game in the 'tweendecks were lining her rails for a last look at their homes in San Francisco — very definitely a last look, in most cases. For, unknown to man,

------

[4]Macarthur, Walter: *Last Days of Sail on the West Coast,* San Francisco, 1929.

[5]Huycke, *op. cit.*

forces already were building up dangerously along the San Andreas Fault, that seismic scar which traverses California from San Francisco to the lower reaches of the muddy Colorado. When *Euterpe* was four days at sea those forces were to let go with cataclysmic violence, and much of San Francisco would be obliterated by earthquake and fire.

About the time that the tug *Sea King* turned them loose and headed back for her berth at Red Stack's wharf, the total of *Euterpe's* personnel was increased by two, as one of the mates flushed a brace of stowaways. Why anyone would want to stow away in a little old bark bound for, of all places, the Nushagak River, is anyone's guess. But there they were, and the captain "persuaded" them to sign the articles. The pay would be two-bits a month, and found.

The first annoyance of the voyage was noted in the log on April 17, the day's record ending with ". . . Julius Unger under Medical treatment by the Captain, for Delerium tremens. Lights, lookout and pumps attended to." April 18, the day of San Francisco's shuddering searing horror, brought them no hint of the disaster taking place only four days' sailing behind them. Aside from Julius and his problem, the log is almost idyllic: "This day commenced with calm and continued so throughout the day . . . Julius Unger delirius through these twenty four hours, and had to have constant guard of two or three men." So light was the wind that on that day they made good only 31 miles. The next day was a little better — 42 miles — but it was noted that "Our patiente J. Unger still desparate Sick and under guard and medical treatment. Lights and Lookout attended to." Did someone forget the pumps?

Julius' recovery was officially logged on April 22, and all seemed well. But squalls were increasing in force and frequency, and at noon April 25 a heavy sea smashed in three deadlights on the port side of her fo'c'sle, bent in two plates and cracked a couple of stringers. It almost seems as if she knew that it was her last voyage as *Euterpe,* and there is something strongly suggestive of her Roaring Forties days about the succeeding log entries: "Day started with heavy squalls from S. W. with Very heavy sea Vessel laboring hard" — "Day started with a storm from N. E. . . . 2 P. M. furled fore and main upper topsails, had to run before the wind . . . vessel acting bad, shipping heavy water" — "Strong wind and heavy seas from Westward, barometer very low." That was on May 11 and she was hove to under storm canvas, with the glass down to 28.96.

Despite an "assist" from the steamer *Nushagak,* which picked her up and towed her through Unimak Pass, this voyage took her 42 days. Wearily, on May 26, the captain closed the account with "Vessel moored and out of commission."

A little over a month later the signature of the President of the United States was to change her name, but that day came and passed without *Euterpe* or her people knowing — or probably even caring — anything about it. She lay there, idly swinging to a swivel from her anchors, until August 19 when down to her marks with canned salmon and with 260 men, she got under way for San Francisco. It was a good passage home, and she did it in 19 days.

Her days under the name she had borne since 1863 now were over. One of the first jobs for the painters was to slap *Star of India* onto her stern and her bows, in bold, yellow letters. Nothing now remained of the old name but the single word EUTERPE incised into the big bell at the break of her fo'c'sle and the little watch bell on her wheelbox. Those were the bells which had marked the passing hours in the high Southern latitudes and in the distant harbors of Dunedin, Calcutta, Port Pirie. One of those bells, the big one, still is there, for the name on a ship's bell, traditionally, is never changed.

Somewhere, in someone's collection of conversation pieces, there is another bell. It is about six inches across, and it is neatly inscribed

EUTERPE
1863

If ever you see this bell you will be safe in calling its possessor a thief — or at best, a receiver of stolen goods.

CHAPTER VII

THAT'S ICE AHEAD, MISTER!

By this time her life had become fairly routine — out from San Francisco for Nushagak in April and back in September, year in and year out. Of course, there were little incidents here and there, like that on her 1907 voyage. That year *Star of India* got to the Nushagak River in safety, and came to an anchor. Ice was heavy, however, and on May 13, exactly a week after her arrival, a huge mass of it came crackling and grinding down the river, rode up onto her anchor chain and carried it away. Luckily, they had not yet sent down her canvas and there were enough men left aboard so that they were able to make sail. After a few hectic hours they reached a safe spot and let go the remaining anchor; finding the original one, and its 50 fathoms of chain, would have to wait until the ice was gone.

The 1909 voyage was no picnic, either. They left on April 10 and by May 1 were through the Pass and up to solid ice, where *Star of Iceland*[1] and an unidentified bark joined them the next day. Then a snowstorm blotted out everything, clearing by May 4 to reveal that they had been joined by the steamer *Kvichak*, as helpless as themselves, and by the barkentine *St. Daniel*. Next to be added to their frustrated group were the wooden ship *Berlin* and their own fleet mate *Star of Italy*. More snow came on May 7, but the ice opened a bit and they got into a little broken water. Another week

---

[1] The former British bark *Willscott* — American registry through the courtesy of Hawaii!

and the whole Bristol Bay fleet was with them, and nothing in sight ahead but solid ice. A gale on May 16 loosened it up and they got through to Nushagak; ice delays had cost them a fortnight's time.

The next year wasn't quite so bad. They made the Pass on May 1, 1910, in foggy weather; it cleared May 5, to reveal ice. At 11 o'clock that night they hit it — and it was solid — but they called all hands on deck, backed the yards and got clear, to play tag with the ice for the next several days, part of the time in company with *Star of Peru*. Through a hodge-podge of fog and ice they finally reached an uneasy anchorage at the mouth of the river. The next day *Nushagak* passed them and someone shouted through a megaphone that *Star of Iceland* was living up to her frigid name again; she was icebound for fair this time, in the Bering Sea.

So much ice was coming down the river that sea watches were set and all hands kept busy freeing, or trying to free, the ship and her anchor chains from the huge, frozen cakes. Snow and increasing winds added to their discomfort on May 21, and to halt dragging they veered 45 fathoms of chain on the starboard anchor, and let go the port one with 30 fathoms. Still she dragged before the gale, and there must have been one of those original mates keeping the log, for it shows that at midnight "shi cammanst tamping on the battam a fiu times and than taking the chain over the wylcat har scalf." A link at a time, the chain went bumping and crashing out across the wildcat[2] of the anchor windlass, until 95 fathoms were gone, on the port anchor. Then the chain snapped, but by a miracle the starboard anchor held. Distress rockets brought *Nushagak* to their aid, and in the morning she was towed out into deep water.

---

[2] The "wildcat" is a notched wheel, or drum, which fits the links of the chain and forms part of the anchor-windlass. Only a terrific strain could pull the chain over it.

62

"Ship Alley" at the foot of Paru Street, Alameda, in 1929; at the left is *Star of Shetland*, at the right is *Star of Finland*.—PHOTO BY AUTHOR

Capt. Woldemar Marzan

Capt. Alexander S. Banks

Capt. Thomas E. Bowling

Capt. Frank Weidemann

Aboard *Centennial* in 1927; First Mate W. Marzan (left) and Second Mate Jack Dickerhoff, who years later was to re-rig *Star of India*.—S. F. MARITIME MUSEUM ASSOCIATION

"The yacht-like *Star of France*" (far right) in winter quarters in 1929; in the foreground is the big bark *Star of Lapland*.—PHOTO BY AUTHOR

In a fresh breeze; looking up at the main topsails and topgallant from a precarious perch on *Star of India's* starboard cat-head.—CAPTAIN OTTO WEIDEMANN

She continued to have her funerals. On the 1909 homeward passage it was logged on September 1 that "1 Chiny-
man died"; he was "berryed" in mountainous seas. A hand
identified as P. Olson died May 7, 1911 just after they passed
Scotch Gap, at the south end of the Pass, and his burial
must have presented a scene worthy of the brush of Gordon
Grant or Charles Robert Patterson. Floating ice dotted the
tumbling, gray sea, and dimly visible through swirling snow-
flakes, the glaciered slopes of Pogromni, at the west end of
Unimak Island, rose as a blurred mass. Briefly the main yards
were backed and she wallowed in icy foam as the ballasted
body went over the side. Snow provided the backdrop also
for the burial of Jose Pearson, who died on the northbound
voyage in 1914. Louis Gilson, another cannery worker, died
on the same voyage, just as they were reaching the river. The
body was taken ashore for burial at Nushagak.

Captains, meanwhile, had come and gone — Christianson,
Swanson, Christensen, Johnson — until the 1914 voyage,
when she went under a master who on one brief and wild
occasion, got 12 knots out of her despite her reduced rig. It
was the only time of which records have been found when
she went so fast, since that glorious day back in '84 when,
under her original rig, she reached that speed and held it for
two full hours. Captain Woldemar Marzan later was described by his former first mate as "a sailor of the old school
— and a gentleman." When the mate speaks that way of the
Old Man, it is the kind of praise which is hard to get.

The day of the old girl's last wild fling was April 25, 1915,
and she was some 250 miles southeast of the Pass. From the
terse entries in the log, it is easy to picture a day on which
they were having anything but a pleasure cruise:

"Fresh breezes gradually increasing after sunset to fresh
gale. Tacked ship. Big SW sea. Tacked ship. Weather cloudy,
rain squalls during the night, partly clearing towards the

63

end of the day.[3] Furled light sails. Lights and lookout attended. Furled main gallant sail and fore upper topsail. Wore ship. Foresail and main upper topsail carried away, furled same. Bent new foresail and set jib. Bent new main upper topsail and furled same. Living quarters, life preservers and fire apparatus in good order — W. Marzan."

During those active 24 hours, clawing their way up through the North Pacific toward Unimak Pass, they must have been at the braces much of the time, for it was noted that they changed course from South by East to North, Northwest; back to South, one-half East; then to South, Southeast; to Southwest, and finally around to West, Northwest. At 3 p.m. she was logging 12 knots — but it lasted only an hour, and with all those changes of course, it wasn't getting her anywhere. When Captain Marzan "brought down the sun" with his sextant at noon and worked up his observation, the result was, to put it mildly, a bit frustrating. She had covered 141 miles of tumbling seas, but had made good toward her destination only 12.

They made their battered way through the Pass and up to the mouth of the Nushagak, where, unwilling to wait for a tardy tug, Captain Marzan showed what kind of sailor he was, by actually sailing her part way up the river. "Sailor of the old school" is right!

A despondent cannery hand named Ramirez gave them a gory and hectic time on the 1918 voyage, which was a sufficiently rough passage anyway. It was around 10 o'clock on the morning of April 18; First Mate Carlson was working up his longitude sight when he heard a commotion, and one of the crew burst into the cabin, with word that he was needed up forward and right now. Leaving his declinations and altitudes and equations of time behind him, he went forward.

[3]Sea time was figured from noon, the time of the observation for latitude, to noon of the following day, which explains why "during the night" preceded "towards the end of the day."

There was a little group gathered around Ramirez, who had attempted suicide by slashing his throat from ear to ear with a straight-edged razor. Now, in addition to taking care of navigation and stowage and handling cases of "sailor trouble," the first mate also was the ship's doctor. Carlson had him carried aft, went to the medicine chest for the needles and catgut, and proceeded to put Ramirez' head back on his shoulders.

The next day they were taken aback in a squall. There was no damage, but as night approached they prudently took in the ring-tail, mizzen-topmast staysail, mainsail and outer jib. A few hours later Ramirez became violent, ripped off the bandages and tore out all of Carlson's careful stitches. All of the catgut having been expended, Carlson had to do a re-tread job on Ramirez' neck with ordinary sewing thread. After the second "operation" they tied him down, for they had no time for further foolishness. Hardly were they through the Pass when they were confronted by ice. They dodged the floes as best they could for five days, in blinding snow squalls, and on May 16, they had no less than 16 other vessels in sight, all having ice problems of their own. The next day, stuck hard and fast, they clewed up and secured all sails. It was no use trying to go on.

Meanwhile the ice was slowly setting them eastward toward the shore. On May 18 they broke loose from the ice but, finding themselves hopelessly embayed, clewed up their sails once more. The water was steadily becoming shallower, and there is a sombre note to the log entries for May 20:

"Light SW'ly winds . . . Every attempt is made to get further in ice in direction away from land. Noon dept water 7 fathoms . . . Vessel hard fast in ice . . . 8: 00 [8 a.m. May 21] Cape Menshikof[4] bore E ½ S, distant 3¾ miles . . .

---

[4]On the northwest coast of the Alaska Peninsula, about 90 miles south of Nushagak.

Saw bark go ashore believed to be the Abner Coburn of Seattle."

Seven fathoms — 42 feet; that meant not much more than 20 feet of water under her keel, and a lee shore less than four miles away. Never had the end been nearer.

It was nip and tuck until the morning of May 28, when the ice loosened and they got a few sails onto her; they now had been dodging ice, or frozen in, for 17 days. That night *Nushagak* got them in tow for a few hours, snaking them through the floes in a blinding fog; at 1:20 in the morning, with only a miserable 35 feet under their keel, they had to anchor again. Drift ice increased and they had to get up their anchor, just as *Nushagak* loomed up in the murk again. This time she got them through and towed them to the anchorage at Naknek — it was hopeless to try for Nushagak, 65 miles to the westerly — and they signalled for a doctor. He came off in a launch and looked over their patient, who was removed shortly afterward by a United States Marshal. It was June 6 before they had enough clear water to the west to leave Naknek under tow, and when they reached Nushagak at last they were 54 days from San Francisco.

That year they didn't start for home until August 28, and although it was downhill all the way, *Star of India* made no more 12-knot spurts; her best day's work was 192 miles, for an 8-knot average. Some hours before dawn of September 21 she anchored off Black Point in San Francisco Bay, and the log closes with a typical wartime entry: "Naval Guard and Custom Officer aboard."

The 1919 voyage was uneventful and it was also Captain Marzan's last as master of *Star of India*. He was promoted to command of the bigger, faster *Star of France;* his relief was a good-natured giant named Frank Weidemann.

By 1920, it was becoming difficult to get square rigger crews, and *Star of India* lay at anchor for many days before receiving her full complement. In fact, she was delayed so long that at last it was decided, her people being aboard at long last, to tow her north. So her old friend *Nushagak* passed her the hawser and away they went on May 5, the latest she had ever left San Francisco. The tow kept on for 17 days, *Star of India* helping out by setting her canvas when the wind was in a favorable quarter. By that time they were up to Cape Sarichef, at the north end of Unimak Pass, and she finished the last three days of the passage on her own.

In mid-August they were homeward bound, on a voyage which was to prove that the race is not always to the swift. *Star of India* and *Star of France* cleared Unimak Pass together, and Captain Marzan, waving cheerily to his old ship, made some appropriate remarks through the megaphone, about beating *Star of India* back to San Francisco. In a growing haze, the two vessels "split tacks" — one standing away on the port tack, the other on the starboard. They did not see each other again, and nothing was further from Captain Weidemann's mind than any idea of the poor, slow little *Star of India* even attempting to catch up with her yacht-like rival. One can imagine his surprise when, on reaching San Francisco, *Star of France* was nowhere in sight. The story is summed up in two days' Shipping Reports in the *San Francisco Chronicle:*

SEPT. 9, 1920

Arrived At This Port

Bark Star of India, Widemann [sic], 23 days from Nushagak, 9:20 a.m. [Sept. 8]; 27,827 cases of salmon to Alaska Packers' Assn.

SEPT. 12, 1920

Shipping Notes

Bringing 15,200 cases of salmon, the Alaska Packers' Assoc. ship Star of France, Captain Marzen [sic] arrived yesterday, 27 days from Bristol Bay.

Weidemann, of course, had found wind where Marzan had not. Several years later, when he was "ship's husband" of the laid-up *Star of Shetland*, he related the tale with obvious relish:

"Yesus!" he chuckled (and there was a lot of him to chuckle) "Vas Marzan mad!"

For the next three years nothing much of interest happened, as the sun of the sailing ship dropped closer and closer to the western horizon. The very drabness of her logs seems to indicate that most of the fire was gone out of her. She was old now, old and rather tired. But the pages are lightened occasionally by mention of old favorites she passed at sea — *Emily F. Whitney, St. Nicholas, Santa Clara, Benj. F. Packard* — last of the Down Easters which had written brilliant, if at times gory, pages in America's maritime history. One wonders if Captain Weidemann sensed, when he sighted the grand old *Packard,* battling the ice of the Bering Sea on May 19, 1921, that this ship would, one day, light the spark which was to save *Star of India.*

On September 5, 1923, Jerry Scanlon, Marine Editor of the *Chronicle,* noted:

"Pier 54 looked like one of the old style docks before the steamship and motorship became so numerous in our port . . . The barkentine Olympic and the ship Star of Lapland of the Alaska Packers fleet were tied up on one side of the dock, while the bark Star of India occupied a berth on the other side. There wasn't a modern steamer in sight."

Star of India had come home August 30 (earliest of all of her many arrivals from Bristol Bay) and had brought 20,300 cases of salmon. The Chinese crew and the Mexican crew and the fishermen-sailors packed up their gear and left. Longshoremen swarmed over and through her, getting out the cargo. Around noon of September 6 the tug *Sea Queen* came alongside to tow her over to Alameda. Late in the afternoon Captain Weidemann, who next year would take out *Star of Iceland*, went over the side after being sure that her last crew — consisting of First Mate V. Turner and four longshoremen — were all through doubling up her mooring lines for the winter.

And gradually the light faded and throughout the ghostly fleet there was silence; she settled down among her companions of the high seas and frozen North, to await an uncertain future. From below her bowsprit, battered old figurehead Euterpe gazed stolidly into the back yards of Alameda. She had come a long ways, and had seen a lot of things, since that autumn afternoon so long ago when she had slid majestically down to the waters of Ramsey Bay. If nostalgic thoughts came to her she gave no outward sign, for after all, she was only a face of wood. A tug churned past; its spreading wake rolled into the Packer's basin, and *Star of India* stirred momentarily. Then, once more, all was still.

She would never sail again.

She would never sail again. As of the time when she came to San Diego, and for years later, that's what everyone thought — but they were proved to be wrong. For as the work of restoration went on there developed a policy of nothing but the best, in materials and workmanship. At times this produced friction within the organization, but in the end the hard-nosed perfectionists won out. When rotted decking was torn up, if an iron beam or diagonal was found to be rusted through, there was no hasty application of a dab of paint and replacing the deck: the offending metal was burned away, a new piece was welded into place and liberally treated with anti-corrosive. Then and not until then, the new decking was bolted down and the seams caulked and payed. It was the same aloft and alow. They were making the old girl strong enough to last, and that wasn't all. The suggestion was made, and carried out, to provide a suit of sails, to display as she lay alongside the Embarcadero. . . .

And so it was that, after great effort by dedicated men, she put to sea for one glorious day under sail, off San Diego. It was on America's bi-centennial, July 4, 1976 — and she was 113 years old. Only half a dozen of her crew of forty volunteers had ever sailed in square rig before, but the exercise came off without a hitch, and from wharves and hillsides and a thousand yachts, San Diego turned out en masse to witness the great event. (See frontispiece).

Part 3 A Fantastic Scheme

CHAPTER VIII

EXIT THE WIND SHIPS

DINNER WAS OVER. A HUGE DRIFTWOOD LOG GLOWED AND sputtered in the fireplace of the San Diego Yacht Club, then located on the Coronado side of San Diego Bay. The muted rumble of the surf came from a few hundred yards away, and somewhere in the growing murk outside a belated killdeer uttered its shrill "Kildeeeee!" as it wheeled on busy wings above a lonely beach.

Gathered around the fire that evening in the late summer of 1925 were a doctor with a flair for showmanship, an oceanographer, an officer of the United States Navy and two newspapermen who had a fondness for old ships. They were there for a purpose, although they were not all clear as to what that purpose was to be.

"Well, gentlemen," said one of them, "We might as well get down to business, and I'm going to start by reading you this clipping from one of last week's papers; it's an A.P. story out of New York . . ."

The story had to do with the *Benj. F. Packard,* a Yankee-built skysail-yarder which had been in the Cape Horn grain trade, and the Alaska fisheries. She now was on the East Coast, about to be burned for her metal when a little group of sail enthusiasts had come to her rescue. The story told of the dream of a maritime museum consisting chiefly of the ship herself; it told of half a dozen old shellbacks who came aboard, hoisted her fading colors two blocks to the tune of

70

"Whiskey For My Johnnie!" and swore that the grand old packet could be saved.

"If New York can do it," he concluded, "why can't San Diego? After all, the sailing ship was an important factor in our history. And we are seeing the end of an era which has lasted for centuries. A few are left, up in San Francisco, and they aren't going to be there forever."

The prediction was true. Even then, from Sausalito to the fresh-water mudflats up around Antioch, there were little clusters of sailing vessels which were all through. Within the next few years the big four-masters *Star of Shetland, Star of Lapland* and *Star of Zealand* — each with *Maru* tacked onto her name — would head westward across the Pacific to the scrap-hungry blast furnaces of Japan. Renamed *Bougainville* and flying the tricolor of France, *Star of Peru* would sail off to Noumea to become a storage hulk. "The Hollywood Navy," that year and the next, would get the last of the Packers' wooden ships, *Bohemia, Indiana, Santa Clara* and *Llewellyn J. Morse*. Within the next four years the Packers would put into service the steamers *Arctic, Bering* and *Lurline* (renaming this old Matson Line favorite *Chirikof*), and would be just about finished with sail.[1]

In the silent films, *Bohemia* and *Indiana* starred in "The Yankee Clipper." So conscientious was Hollywood about technical details in those days that they even re-rigged *Indiana* with single tops'ls, which went out in the 1850s. With a similar respect for authenticity, *Llewellyn J. Morse* was made into a rather convincing *Constitution*[2] for the film "Old Iron-

---

[1] Macarthur, *op. cit.*

[2] Such laudable integrity, alas, did not continue. A few years later Hollywood did one called "Souls at Sea" which was timed for the 1840s. They shamelessly used *Star of Finland*, ex-*Kaiulani*, of 1898, which was obviously a steel vessel with a modern spike bowsprit, double tops'ls and, to compound the felony, double topgallants, which began to show up around 1885.

sides." Later still, *Bohemia* was blown up off the Coronado Islands, for a picture called "Suicide Fleet," and *Indiana* finally rotted away in a back channel of Los Angeles Harbor.

To list the names and fates of all the others would be long and pointless; suffice it to say that they became sawdust barges, sport-fishing barges, gambling barges — or were just simply scrapped, or sunk for use as breakwaters.

But, to return to the five men who sat before that clubhouse fireplace: The time, of course, was the Roaring Twenties, when people had big ideas and, occasionally, were able to carry them through. In the spirit of the times they decided that San Diego, too, would some day have an old square-rigger for a maritime museum. All that this quintette of zealots needed was a ship and the money to buy her and tow her to San Diego.

San Francisco, of course, would be their hunting ground. Within the next few days letters were written, chiefly to the waterfront reporters of Bay area papers, and there slowly emerged an imposing list of one-time Grand Dames of the sea. There were *Dunsyre* and *Golden Gate;* there were *Celtic Monarch* and *Annie M. Reid* and *Mary Dollar* of the steel-hulled windjammers. Of the wooden ships there were *Bohemia* and *Santa Clara* and *Indiana* and *Pactolus*. There were others, too, from powerful four-masted barks down to sisters of half their size, and there came word that most of the Alaska Packers' fleet of "Stars" soon would be on the market.

Having enthusiasm but no money, the little group in San Diego were cautious, and quickly eliminated the bigger vessels, which were bringing $15,000 and even more. Gradually it settled down to three possibilities — *Star of France* at $12,000, *Star of India* at $9,000, and *Santa Clara* at $7,500. Although the only American-built ship in the group, *Santa Clara* was wood, and all five men knew what San Diego's subtropical climate and active marine borers would do to a wooden hull. They looked longingly at *Star of France*, but $12,000 seemed fantastic, and so they settled on *Star of India*.

"Well," said one of the group, as they gathered around the fire on a later night, "now that we have decided on a ship, where do we get $9,000?"

That was, indeed, the question. Various well-heeled civic characters were discussed in a way to make their ears burn ("Him? Sure, he's got lots of it -- and he's keeping it!" "Who — *him?* — He wouldn't pay six bits to see Saint Peter ride a bicycle!") and a lot more of the same. Finally, in a lull —

"How about Jim Coffroth?" A hopeful look went around the little group.

James Wood Coffroth, "Sunny Jim" to millions of sports fans, was at the head of the Agua Caliente Race Track; he had promoted history-making prize fights, and the number of down-on-their-luck sports world figures he had quietly befriended will never be known. With his name as the first on a list of donors, there would be others who would make up the rest of the $9,000. Then a question of some practicability arose: Who knew Sunny Jim well enough to make the touch? The answer came quickly, as the doctor[3] pointed straight at one of the two newspapermen —

"Your dad has known him since the old days in San Francisco. You're it!"

A few days later the luckless parent of the ship-happy reporter sat beside Sunny Jim's desk. A bit diffidently, he finally got around to what he was after. He outlined briefly the plan for a maritime museum built around an old sailing vessel; he told of the selection of the vessel itself and, at last, got down to brass tacks: How would he, James Wood Cof-

---

[3]The late Dr. Harry Wegeforth, who parlayed chicken wire, piano boxes and a few unhappy animals into San Diego's world-renowned Zoo.

froth, go about raising $9,000 for such an enterprise? For some moments, Sunny Jim was silent.

"There's only one way that *I* can think of," he said, as he slowly pulled open a desk drawer and got out a check book. He scribbled industriously, then tore off the slip of paper and handed it to his self-invited guest.

It was a check for $9,000.

*   *   *

"Sweetheart Jack" was on the beach.

At this particular time — it now was 1927 — it was no reflection on a master mariner to be out of work. The national economy was not doing so well; ships were being laid up, and masters with "Any ocean — any tonnage" tickets were going out as first mates or less — and having to like it. The late Captain Walter A. Brunnick did not did not enjoy being out of work any more than he liked being called "Sweetheart Jack." It was a title he had won by being perhaps the only man in West Coast history to be shanghaiied aboard a vessel, not as a 'foremast hand, but as master. It was a yacht called *Sweetheart;* but that, as Kipling used to say, is another story.

Title to *Star of India* had been formally transferred by the Packers to the Zoological Society of San Diego, who were to bring about the construction of a combined aquarium and maritime museum. The Zoo, however, needed its money to buy food for elephants and chimpanzees, rather than to pay its Aquarium Committee's towage bills. Inquiry had revealed that a San Francisco tug would bring her down to San Diego on one of two bases: a flat fee of $1,750, or $325 a day, including the tug's time back to San Francisco. The money was not forthcoming, and grass continued to grow long and lush on *Star of India's* plates, up in Oakland Estuary. Such was the situation when Captain Brunnick called upon the Zoo's president with a proposition. He would go to San

74

Francisco, get a skeleton crew, shop around for cheap towage, and get *Star of India* to San Diego. And he won his point.

The shopping around was productive. The McCormick Steamship Co. had a steam schooner called *Wapama* which, for some vague reason, was equipped with a towing winch. She was going down to San Pedro in a week or so, and *Star of India* could hook on for $500. It would be up to the Zoo to provide the towage from San Pedro to San Diego, about 90 miles away.

In San Francisco, Captain Brunnick ran across one of his Naval Reserve cronies, Lieutenant Commander James H. Willey, and wheedled him into coming along, gratis, as first mate. The two went over to Alameda for a look at their new command. *Star of India,* they saw at once, had not improved with four years of idleness. Years later Willey told the story at the San Francisco Maritime Museum:

"Several days were spent in Oakland Creek getting her ready — I remember we hired some scrub-women and they gave her a good soogeeing-down inside.

"Then a tug took us over to the San Francisco side and we dropped anchor about three ship's lengths off Pier 40. We stayed there for three days — from July 3 through July 5. The fleet came in on the Fourth of July and anchored all around us. We made it a point to run up the colors smartly on the old *Star of India* at the same time they did."

Captain Brunnick, meanwhile, had hired a cook, a donkey man and two sailors. They were now ready for sea — steam in the donkey boiler, a few sacks of coal in the galley, kerosene in the lamps, and plenty of food. Even the water tanks had been topped off, although this was more for ballast than anything else. Willey continued:

"Then the *Wapama* came alongside and passed us a towline. We had the donkey engine for getting in the anchor, but it was damnably hard work with about six men, to go

75

through all the catting and fishing of the anchor[4] with the ancient gear that she had."

They had taken the *Wapama's* towing wire at 10:40 a.m. and had shackled it onto the starboard anchor chain for towing. It was not until 12:10, however, that they had the port anchor up, and were under way at last. The tow down the coast to San Pedro was uneventful, although the spectacle of a steam schooner towing a somewhat dilapidated bark with a Viking ship stowed on skids, must have been startling. The Viking ship had been acquired by the Zoo's president, who on going north to inspect his latest prize, had seen it tucked away in a corner of the Packers' yard. It was a replica, of course, and had lain there since the end of the 1915-16 Exposition in San Francisco. The Packers, had he only known, no doubt were more than happy to be rid of it. He would live to see the day when, in this case, he would envy them. That wretched replica of a Viking ship was too big to keep aboard; off the ship and on the quay it was a prime target for vandals and worse. Finally it was hauled off to Balboa Park. And the night it burned, no tears were shed by the Park Department.

Meanwhile, the vessel's new and puzzled owners had been making overtures to the Commander, Fleet Base at San Pedro — the people who, in those days, had to do with the Navy's tugs and tankers and such — and to the Commandant, Eleventh Naval District, in San Diego. Aboard his flagship at San Pedro the admiral, who was both civic-minded and fond of sail, arranged for the U.S.S. *Tern*, a World War I minesweeper, to take her on to San Diego. Unfortunately,

---

[4] An old-fashioned anchor such as hers is "catted" by slipping the "fish hook" through its ring, and hoisting it up to the cat-head (a heavy timber projecting over the side from just abaft the heel of the bowsprit) and securing it with a chain called a ring-stopper. The "fish hook" is a huge steel hook attached by a wire pennant to the lower block of the fish tackle, a heavy, three-fold purchase slung from the fore topmast-head.

76

he was to hear of this, when the word got back to the commercial tugboat interests.

Around 11 o'clock on the night of her arrival in San Pedro, the secretary of the Zoo's Aquarium Committee was aroused from his slumber by the telephone. It was a long-distance call, collect, from Captain Brunnick. He was in San Pedro, he had cut down expenses by discharging the two sailors, and would someone please send him some volunteers from San Diego, to bring her home?

More calls were made, more wires were pulled. A scratch crew, if you ever saw one, was assembled, and at 8 o'clock the next morning they were clambering into a lumbering old NC flying boat, at the North Island Naval Air Station. The crew consisted of a chief bosn's mate and a chief gunner's mate (shanghaied from Naval Reserve training ship *Eagle 34*), the then postmaster of San Diego, and the committee's secretary. They were flown to San Pedro and placed aboard the anchored *Star of India*.

That afternoon the *Tern* came alongside and passed them the towing wire. Silently, on her last trip on the open sea, *Star of India* headed for San Diego. She passed in, around Point Loma the next morning, and ran into thick fog. They anchored off North Island and, as the fog lifted, the last steam in her now badly leaking donkey boiler was used to raise her anchor for the final time.

Thus, on July 9, 1927, *Star of India* came to San Diego. Ahead of her now lay fond hopes and ambitious dreams; and for the committee a need for aspirin in huge doses. Sightseers eagerly clambered aboard, press photographers had a field day, and, having been a generous host for the last 90 miles, the Navy's *Tern* headed for home.

Back in San Pedro, the poor admiral caught hell. Regardless of motives, it says in the book, the Navy must not "compete with private enterprise."

77

CHAPTER IX ★ ★ ★ ★ ★ ★ ★

SHOWBOAT DAYS

THE ENTHUSIASTIC IF FOOLHARDY COMMITTEE NOW HAD A SHIP, and the chilling thought finally came to them that ships must be maintained.

The board of directors of the Zoological Society of San Diego were not in complete accord with their Aquarium Committee and its zeal. It soon became apparent that any idea of tapping the parent organization for much in the way of paint or cordage was mere whistling in the dark. In fact, they were somewhat perturbed at their president, who had authorized Captain Brunnick's successful mission without bothering to call them into a huddle beforehand.

"The next time you do that, Doctor," their treasurer[1] warned him, with a smile which failed to conceal his grim seriousness, "you may call it a personal donation." And various ghoulish suggestions were voiced about the sale of any items of gear which might help to pay for that tow job. About the only thing which seemed practical was her suit of sails. The Aquarium Committee raised a wail of anguish. They argued, and not unreasonably, that with her sails aboard, there always was the possibility of a movie contract at $100 or so a day.

It was no use. A dealer in building materials saw a chance to store sacked cement out of doors if he had enough heavy canvas to cover it, and offered $600, which was greedily

---

[1]The late A. T. Mercier, who a few years later became President of the Southern Pacific Railway.

Looking down and forward from the main cross-trees as *Star of India* beats the
North Pacific into a welter of white foam.—CAPTAIN OTTO WEIDEMANN

A fantastic deckload; anchored off Long Beach with the "Problem Child," the Viking Ship replica, stowed on her poop.—PHOTO BY AUTHOR

In the first dog-watch; Postmaster Ernest Dort at the wheel, Capt. W. A. Brunnick, and Chief Bos'n's Mate T. Sobieski head for San Diego.—PHOTO BY AUTHOR

Safe at San Diego, and the last muster; left to right are Sobieski, Cross, MacMullen, Capt. Brunnick, Blomme, Sloan and Dort.—DR. H. M. WEGEFORTH

Off Long Beach, California, south bound; with cumbersome gear the anchor is "fished and catted" for the last time.—PHOTO BY AUTHOR

Out of the fog and home from the sea; at the end of the tow down from San Francisco, *Star of India* lies at San Diego's Broadway Pier in 1926.—PHOTO BY AUTHOR

accepted. A truck came alongside and, as the committee watched in sorrow, the sails were hoisted out of the hold. It was well that he never counted them, and so did not discover that the conniving committeemen had "high-graded" from his purchase a jib and a lower tops'l of soft, gray hemp which bore the stencilled three-legged emblem of the Isle of Man, and, for comparison, a cotton upper tops'l, of American make.

The $600, however, was not immediately forthcoming. A bill was sent, but it received no response. A month later there was another bill. Rumors drifted in that the building material outfit was not doing too well, although its head appeared to be eating regularly. Finally the Zoo's manager[2] put on her hat and went down to see him. No, she could not see him. He was extremely busy. No, there was no telling how long he would be tied up. He was in a conference.

"Very well," she said, smiling grimly. "I am very busy, too. But I am going to sit right here until I *can* see him." And she proceeded to do so, but not for long. Someone came out and handed her a check for $600.

The vessel, of course, was open to visitors at 25 cents a head. And there were times when the overhead actually was paid from this source. There were, however, times when it was not. And some of the visitors grumbled that it wasn't a museum at all, but just an empty old ship. This was borne in mind when it was discovered that there was dry rot under the now hopelessly leaky donkey boiler. A marine salvage man was contacted, and the boiler, the donkey engine and the heavy messenger chain with which it drove the anchor windlass, went over the side, at so much a pound for scrap, in return for part of his own collection of maritime relics. Such was the start of the "museum."

---

[2]Mrs. Belle J. Benchley, author of the best seller *My Life in a Man-Made Jungle*.

Now the Depression was on in full blast, and away went any ideas of bringing the project to a successful climax. Hopes, however, remained high, and when a local veterans' organization offered to raise money by putting on Gilbert & Sullivan's "Pinafore" right aboard ship, the scheme was seized upon with enthusiasm.

The cast was selected, rehearsals began, and when the time for the show arrived, *Star of India* was towed over to B Street Pier, where temporary seats were placed. Everyone worked at top speed; she was decorated, floodlights were set up, and on the night of the performance, all hands were delighted to see that practically every one of the seats was filled.

The satisfaction was of short life. Money collected at the gate failed, by a wide margin, to account for all of those filled seats. Then the amateur producers began eyeing the audience critically, and it suddenly dawned upon them that it was far from being a typical group of light opera patrons. Too late, someone discovered that while it was easy to pay your way and go in, it was just as easy to sneak around an unguarded side of the pier shed and get in for free.

When the bills were all paid, "Pinafore" had netted $4.85.

It was not long after this that the berth *Star of India* had occupied, on the Embarcadero at the foot of Ash Street, was needed for commercial purposes, and she was towed down to the "South Front," near the foot of State Street. Now she was on an unpaved road, far from any normal walk-in traffic, and the receipts hit a new low. The Maritime Research Society of San Diego had been organized meanwhile, and tried to help. From their own slim treasury they bought material for new ratlines; they bought a few balls of marline — which, with the paint and other material which they wheedled or brazenly stole from visiting freighters, was about all that stood between her and slow dissolution. The light-fingered proclivities of this worthy group, in the matter of unguarded paint, hardware and bosn's stores, soon came to be tied with the size of the society's membership. By their by-laws they were (and still are) limited to 40 members, that being the extreme capacity of *Star of India's* cabin. Small-minded people began to refer to them as "The Forty Thieves."

Numerous ideas for recouping her waning fortunes were considered. It was suggested that people would gladly pay for the privilege of holding "pirate" and other dreadful kinds of parties aboard. The parties which were of an acceptable kind proved to be in the minority. There was, for instance, the high school party which was to be so very, very nice — and where everything was done short of actually scuttling the ship. The next day they discovered that this particular school was, by and large, a school for "problem" pupils.

Then came word that the Naval Reserve was about to be booted out of the abandoned fish cannery which, in piping times of peace, had proven to be all that the federal government was willing to give it as an armory. Why not an armory[3] aboard an actual, floating vessel? The thought was received favorably, and a committee came aboard to map out space arrangements. They drew sketches and wrote notes and reports. This stateroom would do nicely as the Commanding Officer's office; this one would do for the Executive Officer and the skipper's yeoman would fit nicely into this other one. Space was earmarked for the Pay Office, for the Communications Office and so on. When it was all done, there was one stateroom left over. This would be the Maritime Museum, and it could be open to the public on Saturday afternoons and Sundays; the rest of the vessel, obviously, would be Out of Bounds for visitors. The Naval Reserve was thanked for its interest and invited to go on house hunting.

---

[3]This was before armories, like everything else, came to be referred to as "centers."

Various night club schemes were advanced, but were discarded as their backers were found to have too close connections with the bootlegging set. This was, of course, before the repeal of what was jokingly called Prohibition.

What was intended as a genuine help appeared when the local Chamber of Commerce appointed a committee to "do something about the *Star of India*." San Diego is a Navy town, and it was not surprising, therefore, to find the committee made up almost exclusively of retired naval officers; its "minority group" consisted of an old square-rigger man, and the secretary of the Zoo's Aquarium Committee. The rest had enthusiasm, coupled with an almost blissful ignorance of merchant sailing ships and of sailing ship life. The committee held an organizational meeting, and a subcommittee was appointed to make a survey of the vessel and report its recommendations.

Now, in the average sailing vessel, there is what may be termed a shoestring economy. They are always undermanned, there is never enough in money or supplies to do the job, and life becomes a battle of improvisations. In the Navy there are larger crews and, despite the exasperations of red-tape procedure and congressional penuriousness, it is easier to get what is really needed than in an impoverished wind ship. The report of the subcommittee, therefore, was distinctly colored by service protocol and by "big operation" thinking.

Trimmed to its essentials, the subcommittee's recommendation was that all of her spars and rigging should be removed, and a huge shed should be built over her. This was because, in her present state, she was "in ordinary" rather than in full commission — and it was improper for a vessel "in ordinary" to have her masts and spars in place. The shed, would, of course, protect her decks from weathering. And in this condition, it was their opinion that with a minimum crew of twenty men and a sizable allowance of paint, lye, brushes, scrapers and what not, she could be kept from further deterioration.

The report was received and filed. Happily, the committee did not meet again.

CHAPTER X ★ ★ ★ ★ ★ ★ ★

SHIP OF ILL-REPUTE

"I KNOW THE SHIP WELL. I WAS SHANGHAIED ABOARD HER IN New York Harbor in 1901," read the letter from the stranger who wrote in to ask for the job of caretaker aboard *Star of India* — a billet which chanced, at the moment, to be open.

The committee's outstanding showman was delighted.

"It's wonderful!" he said, "Why, here is a man who not only sailed in this ship, *he was shanghaied aboard her!* Just think of the publicity!"

"But in 1901," a more cautious committeeman replied, "she was on the Pacific Coast. As a matter of fact, she was never in New York at all. At any time. Including 1901."

"Oh, shush! Don't always be so practical! Why, you just haven't any imagination. And beside that, who'll ever know the difference?"

And so, the showman having by far the strongest personality of anyone on the committee, the man was hired; he was only one of a fairly long line of caretakers who ranged from the sublime to the ridiculous. An old sailing vessel seems to attract men who sailed in *Flying Cloud* or *Cutty Sark* or maybe even with Columbus; not infrequently they wear beards and/or turtle-neck sweaters and/or pea jackets, topped off perhaps with an aged and unclean sou'wester. It is not unknown for them to have noses which are red, and not from exposure to the elements.

Under the aegis of *Star of India's* allegedly shanghaied caretaker, her owners were shocked to learn one day, through

84

a story in a local paper, that she had been a slaver. There was a dent in the forward side of her mainmast, it said, which was put there by a shot from a pursuing British gunboat, off the coast of Africa. The secretary of the committee, quickly surmising who had given out the story, spoke to the caretaker about the sin of untruthfulness.

"Why, of course she was a blackbirder!" he replied. "She used to go around to Nairobi and pick up slaves and sell 'em! Not only that, but — Hmmm! Look!" and he pointed up, into the rigging. "See that inboard stirrup on the starboard footrope of the main lower tops'l yard? Looks like it's about to come adrift! Must get aloft and fix it!" And he was gone, scampering up the ratlines like a happy baboon. The secretary sighed, and left.

According to the next story, she had been a convict ship; and there were other lurid tales. Each time they got ready to sack him, however, he would do something superb, like single-handedly tarring down all of the rigging, and the storm would blow over.

Old ships not only attract old mariners, they attract Sea Scouts as well. Hardly were *Star of India's* moorings doubled up when they moved aboard, bag and baggage. They decided to make a civic project out of cleaning up and repainting the staterooms, under the poop, and they turned to with a right good will. This gave the caretaker ideas, and when the first room was finished, one of his relatives moved aboard, and into that nice, freshly painted stateroom. The boys said nothing, and got busy on another stateroom. It was finished — and Relative No. 2 came up the gangplank with all his gear. This sort of thing developed, before long, strained relations, and the secretary of the ship's committee now found that he had an added chore, that of settling disputes between the caretaker and "Those damn boys!" Meanwhile the afterguard grew, until there was such a concentration of ". . . his sisters and his cousins, who he numbers by the dozens," that life under the poop became unbearable for all. More in anger than in sorrow, the caretaker and his assorted kinfolk departed.

Later came a quiet, serious chap with an innocent face and some sea experience. He was neat and tidy, and reasonably industrious. Everything went along smoothly until the warm summer day when the secretary of the committee decided to pay a visit to the ship. He found the deck deserted, as were the deckhouse, the cabin, and the caretaker's quarters. Puzzled, he went below, and there, in the 'tweendeck, stood the caretaker. He was just abaft the open main hatch and with a cherubic smile on his face, was looking at the row of ports along the port side. The secretary looked too — and all but swooned. The half-inch plate glass in each of them was smashed to jagged shards.

"How — how did they get broken?" he gasped.

"With a sledge-hammer," came the soft reply. "For ventilation. It was God's will."

Of course, there were fine ones, too. There was rough, tough old Gus Larson, who as a boy in the little bark *Vega*, out of Trondhjem, had gone through the choking hell of Krakatao in 1883. His own training having been of the most rugged sort, he could never quite understand the Sea Scouts, and witnessed each new caper on their part with a sad shaking of the head and a muttered "Yumpin' Yesus!" As well as a good rigger, he was a good carpenter; it was he who, unaided, removed the badly dry-rotted charthouse which Captain Marzan had put onto her in 1918, when the original scuttle over the companionway developed incurable leaks. There was Bert Shankland, a boatswain's mate of the old school (and more recently the retired captain of the city's fireboat) who could out-splice and out-tie anyone in town, and whose work aloft was done with permanence in mind.

And there was Ed Fox, former chief officer in Matson steamships, and before that — long before — a veteran of the Navy's sail-trained apprentice system. Ed died in harness and was succeeded by his able niece, Grace Hoff, who both ran the ship and cared for him in his failing days, and who could write a book herself about her seventeen years aboard a dying ship. The owners now being stony-broke, these two dipped into their own modest income for repairs of an urgent nature. Such dedicated souls as these made life endurable for the harrassed people who looked to the vessel's future with uncertainty.

And now comes the chapter in her life which would have caused everyone from the bishop at Ramsey to the most junior of her third mates, to have winced, or screamed or, as the case may be, turned over in his grave — and for this the scene shifts to the press room of the old Police Station on lower Second Avenue; the principal character becomes Detective Sergeant Mike Shea, a tradition of the San Diego Police Department. He was fearless, he was incorruptible — and his technique was the Direct Approach. A lot of people took a dim view of him, but you couldn't blame Mike for that. When one has the dismal chore of heading up the Vice Squad it is bad enough; when that assignment is in such a dark period as that of Prohibition, it is small wonder he made many enemies. Let us hope that he gained some satisfaction from the type of characters who did not like him; by and large, they were a sorry lot.

One quiet afternoon Mike and his partner dropped into the press room in that old rats' nest of a station. The secretary of the ship's committee (and as such the owners' representative in matters pertaining to the *Star of India*) was at that time the police reporter for one of the local dailies. Somehow, he sensed that Mike's visit was not entirely social, and this suspicion was not quieted even by the sergeant's elaborate attempt at being conversational about the weather and about how good a chance the Giants might have for winning the pennant this year. Finally Mike ran out of small talk and became blunt and candid.

"You got anything to do with the *Star of India?* Yaa? Well — know anything about that bird you got on there as caretaker?"

The reporter thought. Not too long before, the little watch bell from the wheelbox had been stolen. Then the telltale compass which had been screwed to the overhead above the master's bunk had vanished. Could this have anything to do with Mike Shea's visit? Had the police recovered the bell, or the compass? But no — that would have been by someone on the Petty Larceny detail, or Pawnshops. A chilling thought began to take form.

"Well," said the reporter-secretary, cautiously, "I don't know too much about him, but I've had some disturbing thoughts about what kind of a watchman he is, if people can rob us blind, right under his nose. Why?"

"Hmmph! Ever go down around the ship late at night? You know, that's a pretty lonesome place where she is now — dirt street, no street lights near, maybe a car goes by every half hour or so after 8 or 9 o'clock. It's sure off the beaten track."

"No, I hardly ever go past there at night. Why? Is there anything wrong?"

"Is there anything wrong?" said the detective, in what was almost a pitiful bleat. "Is there anything wrong you ask? Hell! I'll say there's something wrong! Maybe you don't know about it, but believe me, all the taxi drivers in town have got the word! You want to know what's going on there late at night? Okay, I'll just tell you what's going on! There is 'entertainment' — of a sort — going on. And it involves young ladies, if you care to call them that. It's the kind of a

88

deal that's right down *my* alley, and it goes on just about every night except the night when the Sea Scouts are on board and he doesn't dare!"

In the grim silence which followed the explosion of this little depth charge, Mike and his partner got up and walked across the room. Half way through the door, he turned:

"Look," he said, "I don't want to make a great big stink about it and pull a raid and all that sort of thing. It'd get into the papers and there'd be hell to pay. But we're getting too many beefs about it, and it's got to stop. That's why I came to see you, first. I'll give you two or three days."

And Detective Sergeant Shea and his partner were gone. So, within a matter of hours, was the caretaker.

OLD LADY DOWN ON HER LUCK

As THE ROARING TWENTIES GAVE WAY TO THE DISMAL THIR-
ties, Irish Pennants became more numerous in *Star of India's*
rigging; for those who came in late it may be explained that
an Irish pennant is a loose piece of rope or marline which
should be securely fastened down but isn't, and hence flutters
gloomily in the wind. It was an era in which the silence was
broken only by the soft rustle of banks folding up one after
another; bread lines grew longer and grimmer, and all too
often yesterday's bond salesman could be seen standing on
a street corner, selling apples. Such times are not auspicious
for civic projects, such as an aquarium or a maritime museum.

Under such lowering skies, the Works Projects Administration was formed, and Federal funds were poured out to
provide employment for the jobless thousands. By now, our
Iron Lady was but a caricature of her former proud self.
Paint, shouldered out of place by rust, was popping off of
her sides in huge flakes. Cordage was dry and sunburned,
and her decks leaked like a sieve. San Diego, which originally
had taken the old vessel to her bosom, now was calling her
a Civic Disgrace — which indeed she was. Disturbing to her
loyal adherents was the growing sentiment that she should
be towed out to sea and used as a target, either for Navy
gunfire or for the bombs of the Army Air Force. Then Cap-

tain Joe Brennan, who at that time was Port Director for the Port of San Diego, pulled the necessary wires and had her designated as a "worthwhile project" under the WPA.

The WPA workers were eager, enthusiastic — and strictly landsmen. Having cleaned off her rusty sides with chipping hammers before red-leading and painting her, they then turned to on the soft wood sides of her deckhouse, using the same tools. At least they did until Ed Fox stopped them, for a chipping hammer will quickly ruin anything but hard metal. Deck seams, to be repaired, are recaulked with oakum and then "payed" with pitch applied, hot, from a funnel-shaped container called a pitch-payer. He asked them if they knew how to "pay" seams and, receiving an affirmative answer, he went ashore to attend to some business. When he came back he found them happily pouring hot pitch out of a bucket, making a great, black puddle on the bare pine planking of the poop, and sloshing it around with swabs. However, their intentions were of the best, and the WPA "restoration" at least kept the "Let's Use Her for a Target" people off of the committee's back.

When the WPA project had passed into history, her little group of friends, stubbornly and almost without hope, kept on, stealing a bucket of paint here and a ball of marline there, and puttering away at odd jobs of preservation. Sometimes these jobs were rewarding. There was, for instance, the case of the bulkhead which, in those days, divided her cabin into two sections. Its after side was hardwood, its forward side was tongue-and-groove pine, and it seemed, somehow, to be out of place. Just the same, no one dared to remove it; suppose it were original? Then the British motorship *Limerick* came into port and her master visited the aging relic; in his youth he had known her, as *Euterpe*. He strode into the cabin and stopped short, glaring at that bulkhead —

91

"My word!" he sputtered, "Who put that wretched thing there?"

The next day, still with some misgivings, eager hands fell to on that bulkhead, with chisel and wrecking bar. The pine planking was ripped off to reveal that, between it and the hardwood, the bulkhead was insulated with many thicknesses of newspapers. Here, indeed, was a possible clue to its age, and Bob Sterling, head of the wrecking crew, leaped upon the tattered pages. They proved to be issues of the San Francisco *Bulletin* and the dates were all in 1916. The hardwood part then was moved forward and installed. Once more, she had the long, original cabin with which she was launched in 1863.

Then, there was the case of the binnacle stand for the standard compass. Its base obviously was some kind of hardwood, and the square, box-like structure on top of it seemed out of keeping. Bert Shankland, at that time the caretaker, rather surreptitiously peeled off a sliver with his knife; it was California redwood. Now sure that he was on the right track, he got a chisel and hammer and ripped away those thin boards, to reveal a beautifully turned and fluted column of solid teak, around the top of which, in dingy brass letters, was the Latin inscription *Domine Dirigenos* — The Master Leads Us. Why the Packers covered it will never be known, but it is pleasant to conjecture that they did so to protect it for someone, far in the future, who would appreciate its classical beauty.

Such things, however, were mere flashes in the pan; by and large she kept going down hill. The "Forty Thieves" continued to appropriate anything which was not nailed down along the waterfront, and these items would mysteriously find their way aboard *Star of India;* it was like pouring water down a scupper. The Sea Scouts did a bit of "rattling down" and other work aloft, using material of obscure origin, but even this was something like whistling in the dark. Half-hearted attempts were made at renting the ship for parties, with results which frequently were more startling than pleasant. There was, for instance, the time when some lusty 'teenager, following the precept that the growing child must learn to expand his ego, found the handle of the seacock in her forepeak. The next morning she was down by the head, her whole chain locker full of water, and only her stout collision bulkhead saved her from disaster. With right good will, the Sea Scouts turned to, reversed the anchor windlass and, marching round and round the capstan, rousted all of her anchor chain up on deck, so that a salvage pump could be brought aboard to get rid of the water — and the seacock, whose control had jammed hopelessly, could be closed.

Up north, things were going from bad to worse for the remnants of the West Coast's once splendid sailing fleets. In 1929 *Star of Alaska* and *Star of Holland* left San Francisco for the last time under sail; the following year *Star of Alaska* went to Bristol Bay again, but this time she was towed up and back, a dismal anticlimax to the lusty days of little more than a decade before. Not too long after that, *Star of Alaska* was sold for a barnstorming venture and, renamed *Pacific Queen*, visited San Diego in 1936, to be moored just astern of *Star of India*. Once more, *Star of India* had the companionship of one of her sisters of the ice of Bristol Bay.

By this time, her tired, old yards were beginning to sag; a crack in her main topmast got worse, and the main royal yard rotted through at the slings and hung down dismally, like two huge clubs, from her slings, until the Sea Scouts went aloft and got the pieces down on deck. Improvisations with hemp line, telephone guy-wire cable and even bits of clothesline began to appear throughout her rigging.

Then came Pearl Harbor, and San Diego became, overnight, both an armed camp and a major source of aircraft.

93

Luxury liners, now a dull blue-gray, came into port and loaded thousands of troops. The city learned about blackouts, anti-aircraft batteries everywhere, barrage balloons, and rationing. There was no time now to think of a jaded old bark, now all but deserted and forgotten — at least, not to think of her in terms of restoration. People did think of her, however, in other ways.

One who thought of her, as the war dragged on and scrap metal was at a premium, was a man of unquestioned patriotism, and a leader in the community. What a fine thing, he said, it would be to take that disgraceful old ship and cut her up to feed the hungry blast furnaces; she contained, he reported to appropriate authorities, some 6,000 tons of the finest steel. And with that, certain wheels within the Federal government began to spin. A surveyor was sent down from Los Angeles to look into the availability of *Star of India* as a source of scrap.

The first thing which he reported back, of course, was that she wasn't steel at all; she was iron, and weighed far less than 6,000 tons. He added that the cost of cutting her up would be prohibitive, even in wartime, and dropped a dark hint that about all that they would get out of her would be some hundreds of tons of rust. The scrap hunters dropped her like a hot potato. Months later, when the danger was definitely past, the surveyor ran across one of her loyal friends, and the man all but wept on his shoulder.

"I guess it's all off for the old girl now," he remarked, sadly. "We didn't realize that she was so far gone!"

The surveyor looked around to see if there were any microphones in sight. Then he whispered out of the side of his mouth —

"Shut up, you idiot! She's as fit as a fiddle! Do you think I'd be a party to having that grand old lady cut up with torches, war or no war? Those people are maniacs! The man

94

who'd suggest a thing like that ought to be strung up by the thumbs, or keel-hauled, or both! You just sit tight until the war's over; some day, mark my word, people with a little sense will do the right thing by her. You've got a gem, in that old hulk."

And hulk was, before long, just about what she became. The training of aircraft pilots became a major activity, and planes began coming closer and closer to her tall, if neglected, masts and yards. A board of Naval officers was directed to look into the matter, and they lost no time in declaring her a menace to aerial navigation.

The Navy requested, formally, permission from the Zoological Society, her owners, to remove the masts and spars. During wartime, such a request does not have to openly say "or else" — you can read it between the lines. Meekly, *Star of India's* owners wrote them a letter, giving the permission, but requesting restoration after the war. This was not enough. A new and more grim request finally brought a letter authorizing the removal and disposal of her top-hamper in any way that the Navy saw fit, absolving the Navy of any blame for damages, and agreeing to close the vessel to the public while the work went on. There vanished, forthwith, most of the slender trickle of nickels and dimes which were enough at least to pay her taxes. She was open to visitors only on Sundays.

Of course, it was too much to expect that the "rigging down" party would be experts in matters pertaining to the rigging and spars of a sailing vessel, and a vintage one, at that. Sail, and sail seamanship, had long since become unknown and undesirable words in Naval circles. Sadly Ed Fox and his niece, now alone aboard, awaited the arrival of the men who were to do the work.

The work party proved to be made up largely of Seamen Apprentices, but recently shaken out of the trees in the Deep

95

South; lots of them had never seen salt water before, let alone seen a square-rigger. They were under the direction of a Chief Boatswain's Mate who had spent practically all of his Navy time in destroyers. Any similarity between the gear you find in a destroyer and that which is used in sailing vessels is purely coincidental, in addition to being virtually nonexistent.

With happy abandon and no holds barred, they got to work, taking full advantage of such technological advances since *Euterpe's* launching as, for instance, the acetylene torch. Pins which secured the heavy fittings holding the topgallant masts were rusted fast — so they merely burned through the fittings themselves. Royal backstays, which come from the deck up to the very tops of the royalmasts and then go back down to the deck, would have been cast loose by sail-trained seamen by cutting the throat seizings which clinched them together just below the mast-trucks. These, however, were not sail-trained men, so they cut through the stays themselves, with hack-saws; they did the same thing in letting go the head-stays, which passed through holes in the jibboom and were secured on the under side with hemp seizings. The result, of course, was that this heavy wire rigging was rendered completely useless for any future rerigging, and there would be expensive work ahead for a good marine blacksmith — assuming, of course, that in this day and age, anyone could find a marine blacksmith, good or bad.

Luckily, the Navy did not avail itself of the part of that fatal letter which authorized "disposal" as well as "removal" and the unhappy caretaker talked them into rolling up the mangled stays, which he carefully tagged for future identification, and stowed them in the lower hold. He also kept the committee members advised as to each outlandish bit of "sailorizing" by that industrious but untrained group of bluejackets. Despite the fact that legal liability had been skillfully averted by the "hold blameless" part of the letter which *Star of India's* owners had signed, a Congressional committee was to hear of this, some fifteen years later.

Although they hated to leave her alone — and understandably[1] — there was no percentage in staying aboard while the Navy men were taking her apart, and *Star of India's* "crew" took jobs in an aircraft factory. They were aboard only to sleep and rest up a bit for the next tour of duty in riveting bombers and patrol planes.

The dismal chore lasted for five weeks. Out of all that fairly large group of sailors, there were only two who were willing to go aloft; both had been riggers before joining the colors. They were, however, a hardy pair. One day, one of them dropped a steel marlinespike, which went clear through the hand of his partner, working some feet below him. This was in the morning; they called an ambulance and rushed him to the Naval Hospital. That afternoon, his hand a ball of bandages, he was back on board, working with the remaining good hand.

With sadness, and it was not sadness because they were leaving, Ed Fox and Grace Hoff finally watched the "rigging-down" party go down the gangplank for the last time, and glanced aloft into that travesty of her rigging. She now was down to her lower masts, and two lower yards.

The ruin was practically complete.

---

[1]On the night of Jan. 22, 1943, disaster had been close. A southeast gale descended upon the bay; a pile driver barge astern of her broke loose, came bumping down onto *Star of India* and carried away her mooring lines. She started gaily down the bay, but luckily brought up on a mudbank after traveling a few hundred yards.

CHAPTER XII   ★   ★   ★   ★   ★   ★   ★

"SHE'S A BLASTED MESS . . ."

SUCH IS THE MAGNETISM OF AN OLD SAILING VESSEL THAT, even as cruelly hulked as she had been, *Star of India* continued to be a moderately successful tourist attraction. For one thing, Harbor Drive now was a part of U. S. Highway 101, right under her lee, so she at least made her taxes and her insurance premiums, from the "drive-in" trade.

Not long after the close of World War II, the Zoological Society, now thoroughly fed up with their floating venture, brought about the formation of the San Diego Aquarium Society. She was turned over to them for a negligible fee, as a more appropriate body to run a ship than a group whose obvious and natural concern was with elephants and giraffes, to say nothing of gnus and aardvarks. They wanted no part of an aquarium, even less of a rusty old ship.

The passing years brought further deterioration, for anything more than the most rugged essentials to keep her afloat and keep her remaining top-hamper from coming down on someone's head, was out of the question. The health of Ed Fox, her long-time caretaker, deteriorated also; he died in 1955 and, no one else apparently being anxious to fill the vacated billet, his niece took over. Out of the slim profits from attendance and from a little shop dealing in sea shells, postcards and the like, she bought a gallon of paint now and then, hired high school boys to put it on, and did probably the most outstanding one-woman job in maritime history, of keeping a ship from going completely to pot.

Outboard, nevertheless, *Star of India* grew increasingly ratty of appearance, and from time to time was seized upon with delight by those who can get their names into print by writing "Letters to the Editor," if not in any other way. Despite the fact that everything which went into her came from the quarters and dimes and nickels collected from visitors, she was even accused of being "a drain on the taxpayers" — that hardy perennial charge of writers to the Agony Column. Again, the idea of using her for a target, or even just towing her out to sea and scuttling her, began to circulate.

By the autumn of 1957, even the thinning ranks of her loyal supporters had become plagued by fear; the end could not be far off. The quarterly dinner meetings of The Forty Thieves, held under the brass lamps of that handsome walnut and maple saloon, began to take on something of the atmosphere of visiting an old and valued friend, whose days are obviously numbered.

Then Captain Alan Villiers came to town.

The veteran author-skipper-owner from the Australian grain races — the last stand of square rig — had but recently brought *Mayflower II* across the Atlantic. Now he had come over from his home in Oxford on a lecture tour, and was in San Diego for a one-night stand. After hearing the lecture and viewing the superb film which accompanied it, a member of the *Star of India* committee brazenly went backstage and, in a manner of speaking, cried on Villiers' shoulder; would he, as a great favor to a total stranger, go down to the waterfront and look at San Diego's own pitiful relic of the brave days of sail? Indeed he would; not only would be happy to advise her decidely unhappy owners, but he had always wanted to "see old *Euterpe*."

Minutes later the telephone of John Bunker, waterfront reporter for *The Evening Tribune*, jangled merrily. He was told that, if he should just happen to be near the *Star of India* the next morning, he just possibly might run into Alan Villiers . . . and if he should chance to have a photographer along . . .

It worked like a charm. Villiers found that Bunker had a knowledge of ships and the sea not always found in today's waterfront reporters; they spoke the same language, and the happy result was that when Bunker's story hit the City Desk of the *Tribune*, it got, in soft thick pencil, the terse notation, "Page 1 — with art."

In the story, neither Villiers nor Bunker pulled any punches. The distinguished visitor was blunt and forthright in what he thought of letting a grand old lady like her get down to the depths of Skid Row, and Bunker played it for all it was worth.

Now, if there is anything which San Diego, from its officials on down, looks upon with an awe which is at times almost pathetic, it is the opinions of out-of-town experts. Here was a man from halfway around the world, and whose name was known from Malmo to Melbourne, saying just what some of the local characters had been saying for years. Of course, nothing happened right at once, but the seed had been planted, and the dreary repetition of "Why don't they take her out and sink her?" now began to change to "Why doesn't someone fix her up?"

These words got, of course, to the ear of John Bate, who had succeeded Captain Brennan as Port Director, and they had a pleasant sound. A man of vision and of action (sometimes called "The Terrible Tempered Mr. Bate"), he saw in his beloved harbor not only a place where ships would come for cargo, but a place which would be attractive to tourists. That, of course, means things for tourists to *see*, and what is more eye-catching than an old Windjammer, all spruced up and in tip-top condition? He called in the port's Business Manager, Carl Reupsch, and his public relations

100

men Henry Roloff and Bill Mockler. They tossed the idea around, and they liked it.

Meanwhile, in San Francisco, a wonderful thing had happened. Forlorn and unkempt, poor old *Pacific Queen*, ex-*Star of Alaska*, lay on the Sausalito mud flats. Her barnstorming career had fizzled out, and no one liked to think of the rapidly approaching day when the wrecker's torches would write "So Ends" the story of another fine old ship. San Francisco, fortunately, has never lacked for men of vision and courage, and a group was formed to do something about it. They rang doorbells, they twisted people's arm, they employed tactics which would have made Jesse James blush — and they raised enough money to buy her. Executives of San Francisco shipyards and steamship lines came to shudder when they saw grim and purposeful members of that committee approaching them, for they knew that it was going to be expensive. But, with at least a show of cheerfulness, they got out their checkbooks and they began to issue orders which had to do with free drydocking, free paint and free tools.

In a stroke of what amounted to pure genius, the late Harry Lundeberg, head of the powerful Seafarers' International Union, was named as a member of the committee.[1] Steamship men who might have bluntly turned down a request from a bank president, would think twice before failing to be sympathetic to a civic cause in which "Lunchbox" Lundeberg was interested. As another example of the effec-

---

[1]The doughty Lundeberg already had saved her, during World War II. Some eager beaver in the Federal government had decided that she would make an awfully nice coal barge after all her rigging, of course, had been hacked away; after the war, they could sell her for scrap. Notified as to the day on which he must turn her over to these ghouls, Frank Kissinger, her owner, was heartsick. Then he thought of telling Lundeberg about it. Lundeberg reached for his telephone, put in a long distance call to the top brass in Washington, and that was the end of *that* little scheme.

tiveness of this *rara avis* among labor chieftains, a Republican, he was able to get the ship over a difficult hump by a pithy communication to the Governor of California (another Republican) when State officials were about to deny her a berth on the San Francisco waterfront.

One morning the phone rang at restoration headquarters — the San Francisco Maritime Museum — and another segment of labor, the shipbuilding trades, offered their services to the decrepit square-rigger. The commodity which they offered was skilled labor, now needed just as badly, if not more so, than money. This priceless contribution, which lasted for a year, was sparked by Mario Grossetti, San Francisco-born business manager of the International Brotherhood of Boilermakers, Iron Shipbuilders & Helpers of America, Shipfitters & Helpers Local No. 9. After the old ship was drydocked and was found strong enough for restoration, not a Saturday nor Sunday nor holiday saw her without a crowd aboard from the various maritime unions — riggers, caulkers, shipwrights and so on — and a loyal corps of executives, salesman, clerks and others outside the labor movement, who responded to the old ship as well. Each of them received, and graciously, a cold sandwich and a few cups of coffee in return for a hard day's work.

In time the job was finished. Sparkling as the day when she left Connell's yard in Glasgow in 1886, and given back her original name of *Balclutha,* she was towed to a berth near Fisherman's Wharf. Overnight, she became one of San Francisco's top tourist attractions.

None of this was lost on Bate, nor on the little group who had, in a manner of speaking, kept *Star of India* afloat for all these dreary years. Nor, apparently, was it lost upon Al Pearce, a reporter on San Diego's semi-weekly *Independent.* "Let's see if we can do something about the old tub," he said, inelegantly, to a member of the hard-bitten committee in San Diego. The committeeman winced at the term, but like the rest of the members, he had long since become used to disparaging, and even insulting, remarks about *Star of India.*

The *Independent* really made a big case of it. There were stories and pictures in every issue, and premature as it admittedly was, the publicity certainly did her no harm. People in San Diego who probably never heard of her before began writing letters to the editor — and now, some of the letters even asked where donations might be sent.

It takes more than publicity, however, to repair a ship whose neglect had been so outstanding. All through the series of articles, which of course died out in time, Bate had been working, as had the ship's committee. He sold the idea to the Harbor Commission, and it was an idea not only for a restored ship, but for a maritime museum on Broadway Pier with the ship alongside. Here, for one thing, neither the Navy nor anyone else could object to having her masts stepped once more; Broadway Pier is right across the street from headquarters of the Eleventh Naval District, a building which is as high as she is. There was, of course, one big question to answer, and the question simply was whether or not *Star of India's* restoration was practicable.

By this time, the success of the *Balclutha* venture was established.[2] Obviously, here was the place to look for sound advice; equally apparent was the fact that the man to give such advice, and to prepare a preliminary survey of the ship was Karl Kortum, director of the San Francisco Maritime Museum and the driving spirit behind the whole *Balclutha* project. Their approach to him received a sympathetic reply:

---

[2]In the first year of her operation, *Balclutha* grossed $92,000, which paid not only her own expenses, and those of the shore-based museum, but left something over to go into the "Bottom Fund" for future major repairs if needed.

His Board of Directors gave him time off for the job, and his fee for the survey would consist only of his hotel bill and his plane fare from and to San Francisco. In due time he arrived, all fixed up with a suit of coveralls, tape measure, hammer, camera, and a dictaphone into which went, each night, the results of his inspection. From the tops of her stumped masts to the stagnant bilge water around the iron ore and rocks and dirt which served her as ballast, he went over every inch of her. She looked pretty bad, but so had *Balclutha*, and Kortum could see, beyond the rust and scale and wasted plates, a fine old ship in the condition which had been hers nearly a century ago. But it was going to take time, money, much labor — and heartaches.

With his gear packed and only minutes left to catch his plane back to San Francisco, Kortum paused for a last friendly look around her decks. There were few if any visitors aboard that day, but Grace Hoff had guests, and just abaft the main hatch, a table was set beneath a huge beach umbrella. He took in the details; the umbrella, the picnic table, the chairs with their chromium-plated frames and their seats of nylon webbing. Sadly he shook his head and started down the gangplank.

"A tea party," he muttered, "on a sinking ship!"

CHAPTER XIII ★ ★ ★ ★ ★ ★ ★

WILL THE BOTTOM FALL OUT — OR IN?

"And one by one our little conclave thinned, passed into other ships and sailed and so away"[1] — and of those five men who had sat before a yacht club fireplace more than thirty years before, only two now remained. Dr. Harry Wegeforth and Captain Wesley Crandall had long since passed on to Fiddler's Green; a third had dropped out of sight, and there were times when the two who were left wondered if their own loyalty to the cause was entirely intelligent.

Once more there was a hint of autumn in the air, and again a group of busy men laid down their normal duties to discuss a maritime museum and a grubby little windjammer, now robbed of the crowning glory of her rigging and spars. This time it was a larger group, and more potent. Selected as chairman of the general committee on restoration was J. A. (Jack) Donnelley, admiralty lawyer, member of the State Board of Pilot Commissioners, and one whose influence in the recent election of California's governor had been far from without significance. To make it even better, he was an avid yachtsman and a man who knew about square rig, and about the Alaskan fisheries. He was an alumnus of the old wooden barkentine *Oriental,* out of Puget Sound.

At his side sat grizzled Vice Admiral George Henderson, United States Navy, retired, now consultant to James S. Copley of the influential and civic-minded Copley Press. Lounging comfortably around the room was a cross section of the Port of San Diego — shipyard executives, boatbuilders, naval

[1]John Masefield.

105

architects, marine surveyors and plain ordinary aficionados of the sea.

"Gentlemen," the low, earnest voice was that of John Bate, "we have an old ship which is priceless, and we have a whale of an idea. However, before we get carried away, there are certain things to bear in mind, and the most important one is simply this: Is she worth saving, or is she already too far gone? I can assure you of this much. The Harbor Commission isn't going to have any part of a ship which has been patched up to serve as a museum, and then, some night, just quietly sinks alongside Broadway Pier."

Here, indeed, was the perfect place for any faint-hearted member to arise and mumble something about an important engagement to play golf with the Third Vice President of the Fourth National Bank. Nobody budged. Instead there built up a lively and purposeful conversation having to do with such things as inclining tests, metacentric height, possible difficulties in welding iron *and* the grim fact that *Star of India* had not seen a drydock in some thirty-six years.

The honor of being the first firm in San Diego to experience what one might call "The *Balclutha*-type strong arm" was the National Steel & Shipbuilding Company, whose president, C. Arnholt Smith, saw to it that a comfortable bed was made ready for the 96-year-old patient. Simultaneously, various contractors, business firms and labor groups were solicited for the needed tools and cash for getting out of her those 360 tons of sour old ballast. Placed in charge of this detail was, of all people, an aviator, Captain Donald B. MacDiarmid, United States Coast Guard, retired.[2]

---

[2] One of the Coast Guard's outstanding "rough water landing" seaplane pilots, MacDiarmid had distinguished himself a few years before by flying up and down snow- and fog-drenched canyons in the mountains back of San Diego, looking for a missing airliner. No other long-endurance aircraft being immediately available that day, he was flying, if you can imagine such a thing, a huge PBM flying boat. The Coast Guard does not employ timid people.

Because the striking of her yards and topmasts was believed to have sufficiently lowered her center of gravity to make the removal of her "standing" ballast perfectly safe, there was no regular inclining test made before that morning when, bright and early, Captain MacDiarmid showed up, along with some thirty-five laborers and a fine array of picks, shovels and wheelbarrows. Trucks, a crane, and a capacious "skip" were ready to haul the ballast away and dump it. At Charlie Hansen's catering establishment uptown, they were starting on the sandwiches and coffee.[3] Everything had been thought of except reading back in the logbooks for that 1900 entry at Newcastle, which would have revealed her extreme tenderness.

Temporary floodlights had been rigged in her lower hold, and on that auspicious Monday morning late in 1959, the gang turned to. Captain MacDiarmid soon found that he had a new problem, a language barrier, for most of the workmen were Mexican, with not too much knowledge of English. When he saw one of them eagerly loading his wheelbarrow to the point where he couldn't push it, he tried to explain, with sign language and a few dimly recalled words of Spanish, that this would not do. A bilingual workman, seeing his difficulty, laid down his shovel with a cheerful grin, and sauntered over to the man with the wheelbarrow:

"*Poco no mucho!*" he said. The erstwhile aircraft pilot quickly got it, and his problems were over. From then on, a too heavy load, or an energy with the pick which he feared would send it right on through the aged plates, would bring something like "Hey! You in the red sweat shirt — *poco no mucho!*" It worked like a charm, and by the end of the first

[3]An indefatigable member of the restoration committee, this tycoon of San Diego catering first went to sea as a cabin boy in a little Danish brig; his last job under canvas was that of first mate in an American four-masted schooner.

day she had come up a good foot or more out of the water. Everyone was happy except Karl Kortum, up in San Francisco. By the grapevine, he had heard of the proposed unballasting without an inclining test, and it upset him; he recalled the tales of three windjammers in West Coast ports, *Earl of Dalhousie, Blairmore* and *Andalena* which also had been upset. He got off a letter to San Diego, Air Mail and Special Delivery. Here again was an opinion by Someone From Out Of Town, and it was ominous. They stopped the work and assembled the pick-and-shovel artists along the keel line.

"Now," came the order, with appropriate translation, "Everybody go over to the port side of the ship!"

They did so. Silently, but quickly and frighteningly, she took a crazy list to port; it was reminiscent of that wild day in the Bay of Bengal in 1865, and at Newcastle in 1900.

"That's enough! Back to the other side!"

It took her forty-five seconds to recover. A frantic call was sent out to the Smith-Rice people, for the hasty loan of a couple of huge concrete blocks weighing a total of some thirty-five tons; the skip was detached from the crane, which now got busy taking off her iron fore- and main-yards — the last two remaining in place on her stumped masts — and unslinging her two big anchors.

The yards went ashore, the concrete blocks and the anchors went down into her lower hold to give her stiffness. Again the workmen were assmbled on her center line and sent over to one side. Again she took a list, but this time it was slow, dignified, and far less pronounced than the first one. And she recovered in five seconds. Removal of the ballast then went on.

A gorgeous autumn sunrise ushered in the morning of November 23, 1959, probably the most important day in her life. Riding grotesquely high in the water, *Star of India* was a busy ship again, as mooring lines were singled up. Once more she was waiting for a tug, a far different tug from the little steamer *Mona's Isle*, which bearded Captain Skillicorn had brought to her aid in Ramsey Bay nearly a century before. This morning it was Captain Jack Paynter, with no bushy beard but with complete self-confidence, who brought the big diesel tug *Pacific Rocket* alongside, to take her away to the shipyard.[3] One of her forward mooring lines gave them a bit of trouble, and impatient men struggled with its kinks and its rust. Then there was a tiny spurt of blue flame against the vivid eastern sky, and a shower of yellow sparks as the severed wire fell away; an acetylene cutting torch had done the job.

Captain Paynter gave the tug "Ahead — dead slow" as they still were a bit dubious about stability. The gap of water between *Star of India* and the spindly wharf widened. Slowly she swung in a half circle and headed up the bay into the rising sun. Aboard anchored repair ships, destroyers, landing craft and attack transports, this relic of bygone years was the center of interest for the sailors of today, from boatswain's mates to radiomen, from quartermasters to sonar operators. The contrast was startling — and cruel. On one hand were the immaculately scrubbed and painted ships of the Navy, on the other hand a rusty little iron hull topped by three scarred stumps of masts, its waterline showing, half a fathom wide, a greenish belt of already stinking shells and slime.

A widespread search having failed to turn up a docking plan for *Star of India*, divers were ready to literally "feel" the keel blocks and bilge blocks into position under her, as she

---

[3]There was something definitely Machiavellian about the appointment of Oakley J. Hall, Jr., of the Star & Crescent Boat Co., as a member of the restoration committee. He soon realized that there lay ahead a good deal of towboat work which his company was going to provide, and for which payment would not even be offered, much less made.

slowly nosed her way into the submerged floating drydock at National Steel. This, her friends all felt, was the critical moment. When the dock rose and her weight, instead of being uniformly supported by water, was concentrated on her keel and bilges, would her tired old plates and frames be able to stand it? Or would there be a horrible Scrrrrunch! as keel and keelson came up inside and the rest of her settled down into a heap of rust — and lawsuits? Once she was high and dry, would bottom plates pop off, one by one? It was a period of profound and earnest fingernail biting.

But up she came, and with never a sound. By late forenoon she was all the way out, and steel-helmeted workmen were attacking that 36-year-old accumulation of marine growth, with big scrapers. Inspection showed that her bottom plates were in remarkably good shape. With the rivets, it was a different story, many of them being so badly pitted that they decided against sandblasting the bottom; scraping and "sandflashing" would have to do. There was, moreover, serious wastage of her thinner plates, at the immersion line. It is at this point, where the sides are continually "between wind and water," that maximum deterioration always takes place.

A strategy meeting was called, in an office just off the drydock. Replating of some sort was definitely indicated, and it posed a problem. Iron plates were not to be had on the West Coast, and it was felt that welding on steel "doublers" would introduce too great a risk of electrolysis, with the two slightly dissimilar metals in close contact. There was a time element involved; aside from building a fleet of huge C-3 freighters for American Export Lines, National Steel was busy in many other ways. There was a definite limit to the time for which that drydock could be tied up for even such an intriguing antique as *Star of India;* anything even approaching a "Man Who Came to Dinner" situation was out of the question.

Shortly after her arrival in San Diego, the municipal fireboat *Bill Kettner* gave her a thorough salt-water bath.—PHOTO BY AUTHOR

After the *Pinafore* fiasco, the tug *Cuyamaca* obligingly took *Star of India* back to the Embarcadero.—PHOTO BY AUTHOR

Under ominous clouds: *Star of India, Pacific Queen* (now *Balclutha*) and *City of Los Angeles,* which later was scrapped in Japan.—PHOTO BY AUTHOR

It didn't take the Sea Scouts long to find *Star of India's* galley, and to round up enough coal for her battered range.—PHOTO BY AUTHOR

Under the glare of searchlights, "*H.M.S. Pinafore*" was a lovely summer night's
show—which netted its producers $4.85.—PHOTO BY AUTHOR

To pay for her tow bill to San Diego, her sails were hoisted out and sold, as the
"Viking" figurehead serenely looked on.—PHOTO BY AUTHOR

As poverty and "Irish Pennants" increased, Grace Hoff, the "one-man crew," became a past mistress of improvisation.—PHOTO BY AUTHOR

Sunset skies; it is 1936 and *Star of India* lies ahead of her old fleet-mate *Pacific Queen* (once *Star of Alaska*, now *Balclutha*) at San Diego.—PHOTO BY AUTHOR

An old fleet-mate joins "The Hollywood Navy"—*Indiana,* re-rigged with single topsails, performs before the cameras.—PHOTO BY AUTHOR

A blazing end for a gallant ship; *Star of India's* fleet-mate *Bohemia* blown up for thrills, in the film "Suicide Fleet."—PHOTO BY AUTHOR

The solution was an ingenious steel belt all around the hull, held out from her iron plates by welded angle iron, and the space in between filled with a rust-inhibiting oil compound. "It looks like hell," said one of the committeemen, "but it's going to save her life. We can start saving up for replacing it with iron 'doublers' some time later."

So the belt went on; her topsides were sandblasted, coated with anti-corrosive, and painted with shiny new black paint, nicely set off by the bright red "boot-topping" above the waterline. The work took far longer than anticipated, and it was not until December 28 that she left the shipyard, some $17,000 in debt. Proudly they towed her back to the Embarcadero — this time right under John Bate's window — to await the next move.

The old girl had made it.

CHAPTER XIV ★ ★ ★ ★ ★ ★ ★

HANDS ACROSS THE SEA

It would be fatuous to declare that *Star of India's* restoration was one of those gala affairs about which everyone is in agreement. There were times when voices rose, when fingers were pointed, and when the icy tones of "Ah, sir, that may be true, but did you take into consideration . . ." were almost too polite.

There was, for instance, a good deal of talk about installing her in Mission Bay[1], a clean but shallow body of water a few miles north of the entrance to San Diego Bay. The Aquarium Society had even obtained a lease on a location in this area. And an eager young promoter had undertaken to raise a large sum of money for building a first class aquarium, with the old vessel moored alongside. For a couple of years this went on; one individual would promise many thousands of dollars, and about that time one who already had promised

---

[1]Originally, and with good reason, it was named Bahia Falsa (False Bay) by the Spaniards some centuries ago. Sailors, going ashore for wood, got lost and came to its shores by mistake; they were rudely shaken when there was no sign of their ship. Assuming that they had been marooned, they started to walk back to the tip of Baja California, hundreds of miles away. After about an hour's march they came to the edge of the real San Diego Bay, and there was their ship. The name False Bay was changed to Mission Bay at the behest of the romanticists, backed up by dedicated boosters to whom the word "false" is incompatible with promotional activities.

a donation would get cold feet. The plans were revised, from time to time. Finally one was presented, and everyone looked in vain for *Star of India;* she just wasn't there. Somewhat timidly, a committeeman asked about this and received the startling reply: "Our plans do not include the *Star of India* at this time." It was about this time that the lease ran out, and it was not renewed. At one point the view was expressed to the vessel's owners that any plan for a maritime museum should be entirely secondary to her use as a clubroom for the Sea Scouts; it was hinted darkly that if this were not done, the owners could consider themselves responsible for any increase in juvenile delinquency in San Diego.

For some months the project stood still because of an honest difference of opinion about ballasting. One group favored making a monolithic pour of cement into her bilges, as being quick and practically without cost, an offer having been made to donate the cement. Equally vehement were those who felt that anything which would prevent any future replacement of plates or frames would be unwise, and urged, even if it were far more costly, the system used in *Balclutha,* where the ballast was stowed on a cribbing of heavy timbers, leaving access to the bilges for periodic inspection.

There was competition, too, and a bit of sniping. Early in the game, there arose the likelihood of having to compete for public support with an earnest group who wanted to tow the aircraft carrier *Enterprise* out to San Diego from the East Coast — a project whose maintenance cost for a single year would have just about paid for all of *Star of India's* restoration. A novelty was introduced into the Agony Column by a man who wanted her scrapped, and the proceeds given to some good charity; she lacked the grace of a clipper ship, he said, and only had single gan'sails. Moreover, she brought to him a memory of human misery and hardship; he was in her, he said, in 1920.

113

Just as the campaign for funds was about to get off the ground — having been held up for months awaiting a U. S. Treasury Department decision as to whether or not donations to this particular non-profit enterprise were tax-deductible — up popped a movement to raise $150,000 to build a replica of the ship of Juan Rodriguez Cabrillo.[2] Even though the actual plans for Cabrillo's caravel remain to be found, and reproducing his vessel would be a matter of pure conjecture, there was a considerable amount of sympathy for this project to honor the man who discovered the California coast in 1542.

Meanwhile Admiral Henderson had made a flying trip to Washington to confer with Navy officials and with San Diego's congressman, Representative Bob Wilson. He explained that *Star of India's* "rigging-down" was the Navy's idea, and not her owners', and that, moreover, there was going to be a lot of extra expense in putting her back in shape, as a result of the manner in which the work had been done. The estimated cost of the job was $23,000, and Wilson introduced a bill in Congress to compensate her owners to that extent. The bill got through its committee without a hitch, was passed by the House of Representatives and went on to the Senate. So once more — fifty-four years after the hassle over changing her name — *Star of India* was up before Congress again. Party lines were forgotten. Wilson, a Republican, received the earnest support of Democratic Senator Clair Engle as well as that of Republican Thomas Kuchel, but it was not enough. It was an election year, the session was nearly over, and along with some 150 other bills, it died without ever reaching the Senate floor.

---

[2] For a good run-down on the wailing and gnashing of teeth resulting from similar projects, see Alexander Crosby Brown's "Some Replicas of Historic Ships" in *The American Neptune,* Vol. XIV (April 1954), pp. 105-114.

Wilson survived the elections of 1960, and early the following year introduced his bill again. This time it went through both houses without a hitch, and the signature of President John F. Kennedy made it law. In anticipation of the forthcoming campaign to raise funds, the Copley Press had sent John Bunker to San Francisco, to do a series of articles on the restoration of *Balclutha*, and her importance as a tourist attraction. Now through their affiliated organization, Copley Productions, they produced a documentary film on *Star of India*. Cleverly planned in two stages, it would serve first as a fund-raising aid, and later as a history of how an old ship was saved.

Determined that the restoration should be as correct historically as was possible, members of the committee had been busy for some time. Just what had she been like before the Packers altered her in 1901, and again in 1918? Letters were sent off, far and wide, and fragments of information began to filter back from across the sea — from Wellington and Auckland and Honolulu — even from Yokohama. Other California newspapers, notably *The San Francisco Chronicle*, *The Oakland Tribune* and *The Province*, of Vancouver, B. C., published requests for information and for photos. Jack McNairn, then with the San Francisco Maritime Museum, ran down old sailors who had served in her, and got their stories on tape. The internationally circulated British magazine *Sea Breezes* picked up leads through letters in its "Slop Chest" section; it seemed that the grand old lady had well-wishers everywhere.

Problems of information, however, were not the only ones; There were structural problems as well. How many of the spars could be used again, and how much, if any, of her iron wire rigging? Would it still be possible to get four-stranded, tarred hemp line for rigging her archaic dead-eyes? How about hambroline, which ship chandlers no longer carry

115

in stock, but of which some 700 pounds were needed for serving[3] her wire rigging?

Another problem was that of her masts. The mizzen, which was wood, seemed sound enough; with the fore and the main, which were hollow iron tubes, it was another story, for in places they were rusted clear through and about all that held them together was the angle iron "stiffeners" riveted to their inside surfaces. One thing was obvious; the masts would have to come out and be laid on the dock, where welders and other repairmen could get at them. The main-topmast was badly checked, but still serviceable, if the cracks were treated and sealed off. There was a bad patch of rot at the heel of the fore-topmast, which was going to call for major surgery. The jibboom and about half of the yards, as well as both of the topgallant and royalmasts looked sound.

About this time it was learned that the old Moore Shipbuilding & Drydock Company, in Oakland, had gone out of business, and that their veteran rigging superintendent, John Dickerhoff, would be available for about ten weeks. The last of the master riggers[4] of sailing vessels who still was young enough to throw stiff and heavy wire around, he would be just the man to plan for *Star of India's* rigging restoration.

---

[3]To protect wire rigging from moisture and resultant rusting, it first is "wormed" by laying small line in the spiral grooves between the strands, to make a smoother surface. It then is "parcelled" by wrapping it in the same direction with long strips of cotton duck (burlap, if you're poor) and finally it is "served" by wrapping it in the opposite direction with hambroline, a three-stranded tarred hemp cord, a little smaller in diameter than a lead pencil. Finally it is well treated with Stockholm tar.

[4]With the passing of years, use of the word "rigger" has become less exact than it used to be. Legally, the man who sets up oil derricks or flagpoles or smokestacks, or hoists a safe up and in through a fourth-story window, is a rigger. It no longer means a man who can plan and produce a "gang" of rigging for a sailing vessel, although he is included with the oil derrick and smokestack people, in increasingly rare cases.

116

Kortum shanghaied him onto a jet plane, and they were in San Diego the night before the crane was due alongside to "pick" the masts.

Dickerhoff, whose grandfather came to California in the clipper ship *Young America* in her post Gold Rush days, had served in the four-masted bark *Moshulu*. He had been mate in the four-masted schooner *Lottie Bennett* and second mate in the barkentine *Centennial*, commanded by Captain Weidemann, last sailing master of *Star of India*, and with Captain Marzan as first mate. He did most of the rerigging of *Balclutha* and, during World War II, all but completely rerigged the four-masted bark *Pamir*, then running as a general cargo carrier between New Zealand and San Francisco and Puget Sound.

With his arrival came a new offer of help. Displaying historical foresight of a kind all too rare today, the Division of Beaches and Parks of the State of California had bought up the three-masted bald-head schooner *C. A. Thayer*, the beam-engine ferryboat *Eureka*, the steam schooner *Wapama* and the hull of the *Alma*, last of the famous old Sacramento River hay schooners. Dickerhoff sailed as mate in the *Thayer* when they brought her to San Francisco from Puget Sound, where one of his shipmates was Harry Dring, *Kaiulani* alumnus and former Ship's Manager aboard *Balclutha*. Dring called attention to the long, empty and completely protected lower deck of the *Eureka*, which would not be ready as an exhibit for some time, and where *Wapama's* rigging had been made up. Why not use it for the major part of *Star of India's* work as well?

So the big derrick barge came alongside, that hot morning late in June of 1961. Tenderly and with great skill the massive iron masts were hoisted out and laid on the dock. A few days later Dickerhoff and volunteer helpers had stripped off the rigging, which was carefully inspected to see what could be salvaged. That which could be used again was carefully rolled up, tagged for identification, and shipped to Oakland where Dickerhoff got busy, assisted by another old windjammer man, "Harry the Undertaker" Nelson.

Aboard a discarded ferryboat, and within a few miles of her old winter quarters on the Oakland Estuary, *Star of India's* rigging was getting a face lift.

Two square-riggers were together at San Diego in the summer of 1966. Behind the bowsprit of the *Star of India* can be seen the spars of the Japanese 4-mast bark *Nippon Maru*, training ship.—MARITIME MUSEUM ASSOCIATION OF SAN DIEGO

You can grow a lot of barnacles in 36 years! The time is 1959 and the scene is
National Steel & Shipbuilding's dock, San Diego.—UNION-TRIBUNE PUBLISHING CO.

Intact after nearly a century; walnut, maple, teak and polished brass in the cabin of *Star of India,* 1961.—UNION-TRIBUNE PUBLISHING CO.

With the inevitable camera and cigar, Karl Kortum moves out for an "action" shot as the masts are removed, in the summer of 1961.—UNION-TRIBUNE PUBLISHING CO.

Back in the water after her 1959 drydocking, *Star of India* displays her new, welded steel girdle to an astonished world.—KARL KORTUM

"It's going to take a lot of work!"—rusted yards, "alligatored" paint, and San Diego's Civic Center reflected in a rain puddle, 1961.—KARL KORTUM

Every century, one should have his portrait painted — and this is just what has been done. The top painting, by an unidentified artist, is by courtesy of the Manx Museum and National Trust, of Ramsey, I. O. M.; it shows her as the British full-rigged ship *Euterpe*. Below is her century-later "official portrait" by the noted marine artist Charles Rossner, showing the *Star of India* as one of the Alaska Packers' fleet, in Unimak Pass.

CHAPTER XV ★ ★ ★ ★ ★ ★ ★

FIRST CENTURY AFLOAT

AND NOW, WITH THE CHECK FOR $23,000 ACTUALLY IN THEIR hands, the "*Star of India* Restoration Committee" was to learn that there are problems other than financial. It had been determined that the ship would be restored to a condition as much like the original as was possible. That meant a painstaking interpretation of the priceless information dug up for them by the Manx Museum, and the interpretation, in view of the many changes which had been wrought in her down through the years, was not easy. A study of where the broad, red pine planks in her cabin were "butted" to the narrower planks of fir, gave an idea of just how much the Packers had added to the length of her poop. This was borne out further by the presence of unmistakable bolt holes in one, and only one, of her poop deck beams; those bolts could only have held the original poop bulkhead of teak. It looked easy – but was it? Skylight and cabin measured approximately what that 98-year old newspaper clipping said they should be, but this was not enough. Just where had those "family staterooms" been located? What was meant by "patent shutters" which protected those four, forgotten plate glass windows?

Where could a suitably authentic heating stove be found for the cabin? Why was the top of this walnut panel level, while that one was cut on a slight angle – if it had not been moved from somewhere else? From where else, incidentally? How could one crowd the pantry and that mysterious "com-

119

bined chartroom and library'" into the short space where the Packers had put bunks for nine fishermen? And there was the crowning frustration of "The Stairs That Lead To Nowhere."

This bizarre bit of carpentry was concealed in a small storeroom which the Packers had built into the lobby abaft the cabin, where stairs led up from the cabin deck, on the port side, to a door in the scuttle which old Gus Larson had built when the Packers' charthouse of 1918 had rotted away, and which used to end by a door opening out onto the starboard side of the poop deck. Under those stairs, cut into the hardwood panels, were unmistakable marks of what looked like two other sets of far older (and better built) steps. They came up, four from each side, to end mysteriously against each other; it didn't make sense.

Kortum, Dickerhoff, all of the committee members, and Captain George Cameron,[1] former square-rigger man who had come to her as caretaker after her drydocking, all stared blankly at those mysterious steps and turned away, muttering. In some way, those tantalizing old steps had to do with the days when they led up from the lobby to a fore-and-aft scuttle just forward of the wheel — but just exactly how, and where had they been? Captain Marzan would have known; so, possibly would have Captain Weidemann and Captain Ole Lee, who had sailed in her many years ago, but they all were dead. The problem was passed to Captain Marzan's

---

[1] A man of unusual modesty, all that he said when he was hired as watchman was "I was donkeyman in the *Star of Scotland*." He did not mention that he held master's papers, unlimited, pilot's papers for every port in southeastern Alaska, that he had sailed in *Kenilworth* and *John Ena* and *Foohng Suey* — all big square-riggers — that he had been torpedoed four times in World War II, or that his last command had been a big C-3 freighter. It came as a cruel shock to the committee when someone came down from Puget Sound and hired him away from his watchman's job, in which he had been priceless, to take command of a tanker in the Alaskan service.

widow, to Captain Weidemann's son, Captain Clifford Weidemann, his nephew, Captain Otto Weidemann, and to Captain Lee's son, Captain George Lee. All were sympathetic, all tried to find the answer, but to no avail. Both *The San Francisco Chronicle* and *The Oakland Tribune* gave space to the restoration committee's problem, with no better results.

Capt. Carl Carlson of San Francisco—he had been *Star of India's* first mate under Captain Marzan—cast a little light on the original after companionway; it had seats on each side of the aft-opening door and there was a clock on the forward bulkhead, which could be seen by the man at the wheel. So this choice little nugget of truth was stowed away for future reference. There were many other problems: From the lower deck of the ferryboat *Eureka* where Dickerhoff and "Harry the Undertaker" were patiently plying marline-spike and serving-mallet, came word that they were running out of hambroline and might have to resort to spun-yarn; it's just about as good, but Dickerhoff, a rugged perfectionist, was unhappy. At last the basic rigging was finished and shipped back to San Diego—but who was going to put it back where it belonged?

Along about this time, the refrigerator-ship *Westgate*, which had been bringing tuna up from Peru, was literally sold out from under the feet of Capt. Kenneth D. Reynard—who, for many years, had loved the rusty, grimy, deteriorating old *Star of India*. It developed that, in addition to being a master mariner he was a rigger, a precision shipwright and a sailmaker. He also was a talented artist, and unbeknown even to himself he would soon be, through bitter necessity, a welder, when he took over as project supervisor.

The surroundings in which he landed, from the relative peace of *Westgate's* bridge, would have horrified Noah, frustrated Donald McKay and sent Henry Kaiser home, talking to himself. The now mastless *Star of India* lay at the Embar-

121

cadero, alongside an acre or so of deadeyes, chain, rusty wire rope, the repaired but yet-to-be sandblasted masts, the rotting old spars and the new ones from Portland, along with iron and wooden items of vague identity.

There were fittings to locate or have made, and people to be hired—for in sharp contrast to their magnificent showing on the *Balclutha* project, organized labor's contribution in San Diego was minimal. Help came from one local of Navy shipyard workers and one of carpenters, and that was about it. With the Navy, luckily, it was different. Many a young sailor spent many a week-end liberty chipping and scraping and sweeping up trash, just for the privilege of spending a night in an uncomfortable bunk aboard an old windjammer. Various Navy and Coast Guard ships and stations sent volunteer work-parties aboard—as did the Down East school-ship *State of Maine*—and the handsome, semi-circular top-platforms on the fore- and main-masts were built by two retired admirals.

Problems continued to arise from every point of the compass. At one time, caulking and pitching the decks came to a halt because *Star of India* had lapped up every gallon of pitch on the West Coast. They ran out of this and they ran out of that—and one grim day Reynard was notified that unless a miracle occurred before 5 p.m. he would have to fire everyone including himself; the "kitty" was down to $400. There was constant conflict between those who felt that a good job is cheapest in the long run, and those who favored the "quick and dirty" approach. And at times the scene was lit by sparks from the contact of believers in strict historical accuracy with those who feel that if you get a Gay Nineties atmosphere, it's good for any period between Miles Standish and Calvin Coolidge.

A lot of brass-rimmed portlights had to be replaced, and it developed that none of the right size are made in America;

they had to come from England, with appropriate fees for brokerage, import duty and whatnot. There had once been a few clinker-built, wooden lifeboats such as a British merchantman would carry — but Karl Kortum had seen them first. A pair finally turned up in British Columbia — and rusting away in Oregon, they found a suitable galley range. It was not cheap — but it cost less than its freight bill to San Diego. Sometimes the luck was good; for instance, when they gleefully ripped off the poop extension which the Packers had built to house fishermen, its decking proved to be sound, and was just about enough to replace the sadly rotted deck of the fo'c'sl head. Other decking—much of it—had to be bought. And clear, 4 x 4 lumber (which is what is used for deck-planks) is not inexpensive, even from a kind-hearted lumber-yard.

The Star of India Auxiliary came into being, founded by Mrs. C. C. Woodworth, wife of the then president of the Maritime Museum Association — and their fund-raising capacity, for things which never could have been afforded otherwise, was fantastic. Their annual Fashion Show, staged with the co-operation of San Diego's leading merchants, became a fixture — as did Charlie Hanson's annual birthday, with appropriate contributions to the ship. Those who regard a Fashion Show as out of place on a sailing-vessel are entitled to their opinion, but those feminine events bought — among many other things — the lifeboats, the galley range, the cabin upholstery and lamps, and the hardwood companionway over the mizzen-hatch, which is the main entrance to the 'tween-decks museum-space.

The Little Iron Lady was far from finished when her hundredth birthday rolled around — but at least she was decently clothed, even for a party of king-size proportions. All of her yards had been crossed, she was freshly painted, there was a safe and adequate gangway, and she even had a

123

few exhibit-pieces. Moreover, a friend had donated canvas and Reynard had made her a beautifully fitting fore lower topsail, to be set on state occasions.

November 14, 1963, just an even century from the day when she slid down the ways in far-off Ramsey, came in with a partly cloudy sky and a hint of possible rain—which, luckily, failed to develop. Crowds began to gather, as did television crews with their cables leading everywhere. Captain Villiers, all the way from England, was there as the honored guest. It was he who read, for the assembled friends and the unseen thousands of TV viewers, the cablegram of congratulation from the Shaw Savill Line, her old owners, and formally presented the Shaw Savill house-flag which they had sent. A congratulatory telegram came in from the Alaska Packers, who also sent a house-flag.

As there was no record of any formal christening when *Euterpe* got her new name of *Star of India*, it had been decided to "make a decent woman of her" on her centennial date. And so, as the sun of late afternoon passed behind a cloud-bank and the nearby municipal fireboat *Louis Almgren* sent up jets of water into the sky, Mrs. Woodworth smashed a be-ribboned bottle of champagne over the capstan on the fo'c'sl-head, and pronounced the words which made the century-old veteran—legally, formally and for all time—*Star of India*.

*   *   *

Restoration has crossed—or has it?—that faint line which separates it from maintenance. The work goes on, and the visitors enjoy nothing more that to watch a professional or a volunteer pitching a deck-seam or taking care of a bit of cordage before it becomes an Irish pennant. For, as the old saying goes, "A ship is never finished until she's sunk!"

APPENDIX

VOYAGES AND MASTERS, *EUTERPE/STAR OF INDIA*

Sailed From		To	Returned To		Master
Liverpool	Jan. 9, 1864	Calcutta	Liverpool	Nov. 15, 1864	Wm. J. Storry
Liverpool	Dec. 31, '64	Calcutta, Colombo, Madras	London	Nov. 29, '66	Wm. J. Storry[1] A. J. Whiteside
London	Feb. 23, '67	Calcutta	London	Jan. 22, '68	Wm. Murton
London	Mar. 25, '68	Colombo, Calcutta	London	Jul. 10, '69	Jno. Kyle
London	Aug. 31, '69	Bombay, Rangoon	London	Oct. 6, '70	Wm. Cozzens
London	Nov. 5, '70	Bombay	Havre	Oct. 4, '71	Wm. Cozzens
London	Dec. 23, '71	Melbourne	London	Oct. 21, '72	Thos. E. Phillips
London	Dec. 4, '72	Dunedin	London[2]	Apr. 10, '74	Thos. E. Phillips
London	Apr. 25, '74	Wellington	Liverpool	Oct. 2, '75	Thos. E. Phillips
London	Dec. 13, '75	Lyttleton	London	Oct. 8, '76	Thos. E. Phillips
London	Dec. 1, '76	Dunedin	London	Apr. 3, '78	Thos. E. Phillips
London	Jul. 5, '78	Dunedin	London	May 23, '79	Thos. E. Phillips
London	Jul. 30, '79	Lyttleton	London	Jun. 30, '80	Thos. E. Phillips
London	Oct. 25, '80	Wellington	London	Sep. 14, '81	Thos. E. Phillips
London	Oct. 19, '81	Wellington	London	Sep. 7, '82	Thos. E. Phillips
London	Oct. 9, '82	Wellington	Liverpool[3]	Mar. 1, '84	Thos. E. Phillips
Glasgow	Apr. 9, '84	Port Chalmers, Napier	London	Apr. 11, '85	Geo. E. Hoyle
London	Jul. 4, '85	Auckland	London	Jun. 26, '86	Geo. E. Hoyle

[1] Dismasted on this voyage; Capt. Storry died en route home, and vessel brought in by mate.
[2] Via San Francisco, Antwerp.   [3] Via San Francisco

VOYAGES AND MASTERS, EUTERPE/STAR OF INDIA (Continued)

Sailed From		To	Returned To		Master
London	Aug. 16, '86	Auckland	London	Aug. 12, '87	Geo. E. Hoyle
London	Oct. 3, '87	Melbourne, Port Chalmers	London	Aug. 7, '88	H. W. Bowman
London	Nov. 3, '88	Wellington, Port Pirie	Hamburg[4]	Mar. 18, '90	Thos. Bowling
Hamburg	May 21, '90	Melbourne, Napier	London	May 2, '91	—— Rule
London	Jul. 13, '91	Wellington	London	May 17, '92	R. Streeter
Glasgow	'92	Port Chalmers, Dunedin	London	Sep. 12, '93	R. Streeter
London, Glasgow	Oct. 4, '93	Dunedin	London	'94	A. S. Banks
Liverpool	Apr. 9, '95	Wellington, Dunedin, Napier	Liverpool	Apr. 30, '96	A. S. Banks
London	Jun. 22, '96	Dunedin	London	'97	A. S. Banks
London, Greenock	Oct. 4, '97	Port Chalmers, Newcastle	Royal Rds, Tacoma	Oct. 5, '98	H. Longmuir
Tacoma	Nov. 20, '98	Port Adelaide, Newcastle	Pt. Townsend	Sep. 8, '99	C. G. Saxe
Port Ludlow	Oct. 30, '99	Fremantle	San Francisco	Dec. 20, 1900	C. G. Saxe
San Francisco	Feb. 10, 1901	Melbourne, Newcastle	San Francisco	Sep. 17, '01	Geo. Swanson
San Francisco	Apr. 17, '02	Nushagak	San Francisco	Sep. 11, '02	Sam Christianson
San Francisco	Apr. 13, '03	Bristol Bay	San Francisco	Sep. 8, '03	Geo. Swanson
San Francisco	Apr. 15, '04	Bristol Bay	San Francisco	Sep. 11, '04	Geo. Swanson

[4]Via Iquique

VOYAGES AND MASTERS, EUTERPE/STAR OF INDIA (Continued)

Sailed From		To	Returned To		Master
San Francisco	Apr. 14, '05	Nushagak	San Francisco	Sep. 16, '05	Geo. Swanson
San Francisco	Apr. 14, '06	Nushagak	San Francisco	Sep. 10, '06	Geo. Swanson
San Francisco	Apr. 8, '07	Nushagak	San Francisco	Sep. 7, '07	S. Christensen
San Francisco	Apr. 10, '08	Nushagak	San Francisco	Sep. 14, '08	S. Christensen
San Francisco	Apr. 10, '09	Nushagak	San Francisco	Sep. 15, '09	S. Christensen
San Francisco	Apr. 13, '10	Nushagak	San Francisco	Sep. 14, '10	S. Christensen
San Francisco	Apr. 12, '11	Nushagak	San Francisco	Sep. 4, '11	S. Christensen
San Francisco	Apr. 14, '12	Nushagak	San Francisco	Sep. 9, '12	S. Christensen
San Francisco	Apr. 11, '13	Nushagak	San Francisco	Sep. 9, '13	R. Johnson
San Francisco	Apr. 10, '14	Nushagak	San Francisco	Sep. 6, '14	W. Marzan
San Francisco	Apr. 10, '15	Nushagak	San Francisco	Sep. 6, '15	W. Marzan
San Francisco	Apr. 8, '16	Nushagak	San Francisco	Sep. 22, '16	W. Marzan
San Francisco	Apr. 10, '17	Nushagak	San Francisco	Sep. 13, '17	W. Marzan
San Francisco	Apr. 10, '18	Nushagak	San Francisco	Sep. 19, '18	W. Marzan
San Francisco	Apr. 15, '19	Nushagak	San Francisco	Sep. 8, '19	W. Marzan
San Francisco	May 5, '20[5]	Nushagak	San Francisco	Sep. 7, '20	F. Weidemann
San Francisco	Apr. 20, '21	Nushagak	San Francisco	Sep. 18, '21	F. Weidemann
San Francisco	Apr. 23, '22	Nushagak	San Francisco	Sep. 6, '22	F. Weidemann
San Francisco	Apr. 29, '23	Nushagak	San Francisco	Aug. 30, '23	F. Weidemann
San Francisco	Jul. 5, '27[6]	San Diego	———	Jul. 7, '27	W. A. Brunnick

[5]In tow Str. *Nushagak*   [6]In tow Str. *Wapama* to San Pedro, U.S.S. *Tern* San Pedro to San Diego.

127

Appendix B — Structural Data

EUTERPE/STAR OF INDIA

Hull: Original register tonnage 1246[1]; length on keel 202 feet, statutory length 205 feet, beam 35 feet, depth of hull 23½ feet; 9-inch bar keel; two decks; two bulkheads, lower part of hull cemented; thickness of plating from garboards to upper part of bilge $^{13}/_{16}''$, from upper part of bilge to sheerstrake $^{11}/_{16}''$; frames spaced 18" from moulding-edge to moulding-edge.

Lloyds' surveys while under construction: Frame June 10, 1863; progress of riveting July 15; beams, before decks laid, Aug. 18; when hull completed, but before coating applied, Sept. 20; after launching, Dec. 15. Final survey held, and certificate issued Jan. 5, 1864 at Ramsey, Isle of Man.

Mainmast: Deck to truck, 124' 8".

Main yard: 72'.

Main lower topsail yard: 66'.

Main upper topsail yard: 60'.

Main topgallant yard: 50'.

Main royal yard: 40'.

Jibboom: 55'.

Loaded draft, 22' aft, 20' forward; light draft 14½' aft, 12½' forward.

---

[1]Original gross tonnage as determined by survey, 1197; underdeck 1107. As altered by the Packers, the tonnages became 1318 gross, 1247 net and 1197 underdeck. Original tonnage of 1246, quoted in *Mona's Herald*, probably was a builders' estimate.

130

83; "night life" aboard, 88-89; proposed scrapping of, 94; rigged down by Navy, 95-97; drydocked, 110; abortive aquarium scheme, 113; federal funds to re-rig, 114; rechristened, 126

Star of India Auxiliary, 123

Star of Italy, 38, 54

Star of Lapland, 57, 71

Star of Peru, 55, 57

Star of Poland, 57

Star of Russia, 39, 54

Star of Scotland, 57

Star of Shetland, 57

Star of Zealand, 57, 71

State of Maine, 122

Steel square-riggers built in U. S., 57

St. Daniel, 61

Steinbek, 57

Sterling, Bob, 92

St. Nicholas, 68

Storms, outstanding, 24, 27, 31

Storry, Capt. W. J., 2, 22, 25; death of, 26

Sutherland, Geo., 13

— T —

T. F. Oakes, 57

Tern, U.S.S., 76-77

Tillie E. Starbuck, 57

Trincomalee, refuge in, 25

Turakina, 19

Turner, V., 69

— V —

Viking Ship replica, 76

Villiers, Capt. Alan, 99, 124

— W —

Wakefield, Nash & Co., 15, 27

Wapama, 75, 177

Wegeforth, Dr. H. M., 72, 105

Weidemann, Capt. Clifford, 121

Weidemann, Capt. Frank, 66-69, 117

Weidemann, Capt. Otto, 121

Westgate, 121

Whiteside, A. J., 26

Willey, Lt. Comdr. J. A., 75

Wm. P. Frye, 57

Willscott, 39

Wilson, Rep. Bob, 114

Woodworth, Mr. & Mrs. C. C., 123

Works Projects Administration, 90

— Y —

Young America, 117

— Z —

Zemindar, 57

133

NUSHAGAK
BRISTOL BAY
NAKNEK
UNIMAK PASS

GLASGOW
BELFAST
RAMSEY

TACOMA
ROYAL ROADS
PORT LUDLOW
PORT TOWNSEND

SAN FRANCISCO
ALAMEDA
SAN DIEGO

LONG BEACH

HONOLULU

KAANAPALI

ATLANTIC
OCEAN

PACIFIC OCEAN

IQUIQUE

ANTARCTIC

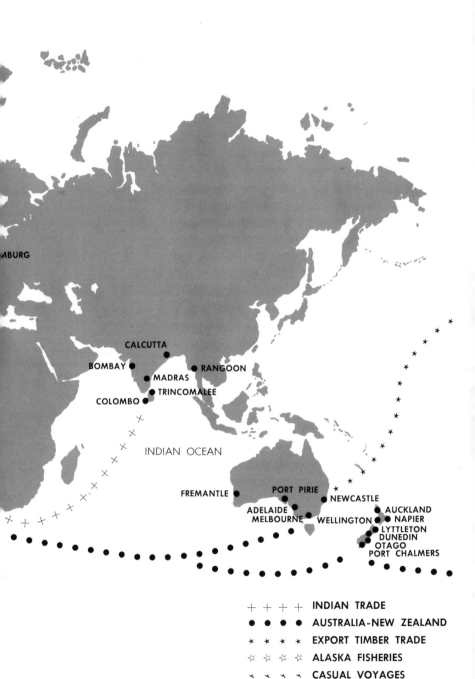

BURG

CALCUTTA

BOMBAY

MADRAS

RANGOON

TRINCOMALEE

COLOMBO

INDIAN OCEAN

FREMANTLE

PORT PIRIE

NEWCASTLE

AUCKLAND

ADELAIDE

NAPIER

MELBOURNE

WELLINGTON

LYTTLETON

DUNEDIN

OTAGO

PORT CHALMERS

+ + + + INDIAN TRADE

● ● ● ● AUSTRALIA-NEW ZEALAND

★ ★ ★ ★ EXPORT TIMBER TRADE

☆ ☆ ☆ ☆ ALASKA FISHERIES

⌇ ⌇ ⌇ ⌇ CASUAL VOYAGES